I0011783

World Bistro Enterprise

Gourmet Genius Evolution

Dr. Masoud Nikravesh

PUBLICATION DATE: APRIL 19

World Bistro Enterprise: Gourmet Genius Evolution

DEDICATION

Dr. Masoud Nikravesh dedicates this book to the advancement of Artificial
General Intelligence (AGI) in the interest of society and humanity,
highlighting a commitment to harness AGI
for the betterment of all.

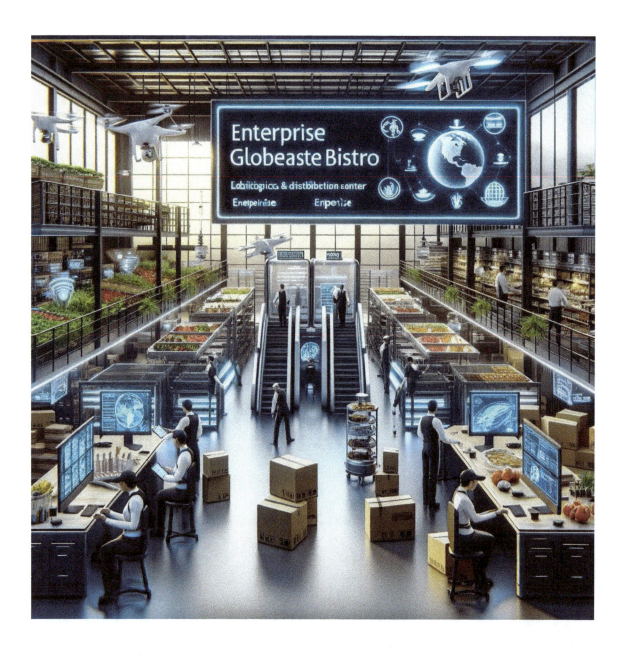

ACKNOWLEDGMENTS

Dr. Nikravesh extends deep gratitude to the individuals and organizations who played a crucial role in developing AI technologies for the betterment of society. The acknowledgments serve as a tribute to their inspiration and support in making this book possible. These cutting-edge technologies were instrumental in shaping the narrative, and the author sincerely appreciates their accessibility to the public, including but not limited to OpenAI's ChatGPT & DALL-E and Midjourney. The realization of this book would not have been possible without these groundbreaking advancements, enriching the narrative and bringing it to life.

World Bistro Enterprise (Gourmet Genius Evolution)

Unleashing the Power of GPT in Culinary Innovation:
The Creation of "Enterprise GlobeTaste Bistro"

In an age where artificial intelligence is revolutionizing industries, the culinary world is not far behind. Enter the groundbreaking capabilities of Generative Pre-trained Transformer (GPT), a sophisticated AI model that has transcended the boundaries of traditional recipe and dish creation to conceptualize something as grand as the "Enterprise GlobeTaste Bistro" – an integrated culinary conglomerate (GlobeTaste Bistro's Restaurant, Catering, Home-Based Food Delivery, and Small to Medium-Scale Food Delivery to global Corporate-Business Food Delivery).

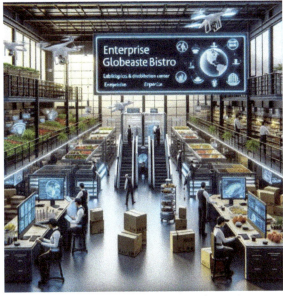

From Digital Chef to Culinary Architect

Initially, GPT's role in the culinary sphere seemed confined to generating recipes or providing cooking tips. However, its evolution has been nothing short of remarkable. This AI model, trained on vast datasets encompassing culinary knowledge, techniques, and business acumen, has demonstrated an uncanny ability to curate high-caliber, budget-friendly recipes from renowned chefs and Michelin-starred restaurants.

But GPT didn't stop there. It took a leap from being a digital chef to a culinary architect, capable of crafting comprehensive business models for diverse restaurant ventures. The creation of "Enterprise GlobeTaste Bistro" is a testament to this remarkable evolution.

The Birth of "Enterprise GlobeTaste Bistro"

"Enterprise GlobeTaste Bistro" is not just a restaurant – it's a conglomeration of five distinct yet interrelated culinary services: a traditional restaurant, a catering service, home-based food delivery, small to medium-scale food delivery, and corporate-business food delivery. Each component is unique in its operation, target market, and revenue model. Yet, under the umbrella of "Enterprise GlobeTaste Bistro," they synergize to create a holistic culinary enterprise.

1

The GPT Touch in Business Integration

The integration of these varied services into a single conglomerate was made possible by GPT's advanced capabilities in market analysis, financial forecasting, and strategic planning. The AI model conducted a detailed financial analysis for each business unit, considering factors like revenue, costs, profit margins, and potential for growth. It then synthesized these analyses to provide a comprehensive financial outlook for the integrated enterprise.

Strategic Enhancements and Financial Projections

GPT identified top strategic enhancements for each business model, ranging from menu optimization and technology integration to marketing strategies and customer engagement. It calculated the potential revenue and profit increases in percentage and dollar values, offering a clear projection of the financial uplift these enhancements could bring.

Navigating the Challenges

Creating "Enterprise GlobeTaste Bistro" was not without challenges. Integrating diverse business models required careful consideration of resource allocation, brand consistency, and operational efficiency. GPT navigated these complexities by providing tailored recommendations for each business model and overarching strategies for the integrated enterprise.

A Vision for the Future

The creation of "Enterprise GlobeTaste Bistro" is just the beginning. It showcases the immense potential of AI like GPT in revolutionizing not just culinary creation but also comprehensive business planning and execution in the food industry. As GPT continues to evolve, its role in culinary innovation and enterprise development is poised to expand, offering exciting possibilities for the future of gastronomy.

In conclusion, the journey of GPT from a digital assistant in recipe generation to the architect behind "Enterprise GlobeTaste Bistro" is a remarkable example of AI's evolving role in creative and strategic industries. It stands as a testament to the untapped potential of AI in transforming ideas into comprehensive, successful business models, heralding a new era in the culinary world.

Gourmet Genius
Culinary Assistant for Quick, Budget-Friendly Recipes from Top Chefs

Gourmet Genius is uniquely designed as a culinary assistant, specializing in offering quick and budget-friendly recipes. What sets it apart are its specific capabilities:

1. **Curation of High-Caliber Recipes:** It pulls recipes and cooking tips primarily from Iron Chef America's executive chefs and Michelin-starred restaurants, ensuring the recommendations are of top-notch quality.

2. **Budget-Friendly Options:** It caters to various budget constraints, providing recipes that can be made for under $20, $15, $10, and even $5 per person. This makes it ideal for users who want gourmet cooking experiences without overspending.

3. **Quick Meal Solutions:** Focusing on dishes that can be prepared within 30 minutes, Gourmet Genius is perfect for those who want delicious meals without a lengthy cooking process.

4. **Detailed Culinary Assistance:** It offers step-by-step cooking instructions, alternative ingredient suggestions, and efficient, cost-effective cooking tips, making it easier for anyone to cook like a top chef.

5. **Visual Culinary Experience:** With the ability to create images of recipe ingredients and final dishes, users can visualize what they're about to cook, enhancing the overall cooking experience.

6. **Chef and Restaurant Specific Recommendations:** Each recipe is linked to specific chefs, restaurants, TV shows, or videos, adding a layer of authenticity and prestige to the cooking advice.

Gourmet Genius is essentially a blend of a gourmet cookbook, a budget-friendly meal planner, and a cooking class, all rolled into one accessible, AI-powered assistant.

3

Gourmet Genius
Classic Spaghetti Aglio e Olio
by Chef Massimo Bottura
Michelin-Star Chef's Recipe Under $10

For a Michelin-star chef's recipe under $10, I recommend a classic **Spaghetti Aglio e Olio.** This simple yet **flavorful Italian dish** is famously prepared by **Chef Massimo Bottura,** known for his three-Michelin-star restaurant Osteria Francescana in Italy. This recipe is cost-effective, quick to prepare, and embodies the essence of high-quality Italian cooking.

Ingredients:

200g Spaghetti Pasta
4-5 cloves of Garlic, thinly sliced
1/2 cup Extra Virgin Olive Oil
1/2 teaspoon Red Pepper Flakes (optional)
Fresh Basil Leaves
1/2 cup freshly grated Parmesan Cheese
Salt, to taste
Freshly ground Black Pepper, to taste
Cherry Tomatoes (optional, for garnish)

Instructions:

Cook the Spaghetti: Bring a large pot of salted water to a boil. Add spaghetti and cook until al dente, about 8-10 minutes. Reserve about a cup of pasta water, then drain.

Prepare the Sauce: While the pasta cooks, heat the olive oil in a large pan over medium heat. Add the sliced garlic and red pepper flakes. Sauté until the garlic is golden brown (be careful not to burn it).

Combine: Add the drained spaghetti to the pan with garlic and oil. Toss well to coat the pasta in the garlic oil. If the pasta seems dry, add a little of the reserved pasta water.

Finish the Dish: Remove the pan from heat. Add the fresh basil, Parmesan cheese, salt, and pepper. Toss again to combine.

Serve: Garnish with fresh basil leaves and cherry tomatoes. Serve immediately.

This dish is a testament to the beauty of simplicity in cooking, something that Chef Bottura often emphasizes. The key is to use the freshest ingredients possible to achieve the best flavor.

Cooking Tips:

Garlic: Slice it thinly for a more subtle flavor.

Pasta Water: It's rich in starch and helps to create a silky sauce that clings to the pasta.

Olive Oil: Use the best quality you can afford, as it's a central flavor component.

Spaghetti Aglio e Olio, inspired by Chef Massimo Bottura. This dish exemplifies the elegance of simplicity in Italian cooking, showcasing the glossy, garlic-infused olive oil coating the al dente spaghetti, enhanced with fresh basil, Parmesan, and a touch of cherry tomatoes for color. It's a perfect example of how a few quality ingredients can create a Michelin-star-worthy meal without breaking the bank. Enjoy your culinary creation!

4

Gourmet Genius
The "Culinary Canvas Concierge" Service

"Culinary Canvas Concierge": This unique feature allows you to upload an image of a dish, and in response, you receive a detailed breakdown of the recipe, including ingredients, step-by-step cooking instructions, diet and nutrition facts, and estimated cost per serving. Additionally, the service provides two custom-generated images: one showcasing the neatly arranged raw ingredients and another depicting the final plated dish. It's a comprehensive culinary guide at your fingertips, ideal for home cooks, food enthusiasts, and culinary professionals alike, seeking inspiration or precise guidance on replicating gourmet dishes.

"Culinary Canvas Concierge" Example:

The image you've uploaded is of a classic dish, Spaghetti Aglio e Olio with cherry tomatoes and basil. This is a traditional Italian pasta dish from Naples, known for its simplicity and quick preparation time. It's typically made with just spaghetti, sliced garlic, olive oil, and sometimes a sprinkle of chili flakes, all topped with Parmesan cheese and fresh herbs.

Here's a recipe for a single serving that should cost under $10:

Ingredients:

Spaghetti, 100g ($0.50)
Extra-virgin olive oil, 2 tablespoons ($0.40)
Fresh garlic, 2 cloves, thinly sliced ($0.10)
Cherry tomatoes, a handful, halved ($0.50)
Fresh basil leaves, a small bunch ($0.50)
Grated Parmesan cheese, 1 tablespoon ($0.50)
Salt and pepper to taste
Red pepper flakes (optional)

Cooking Guide:

Cook the spaghetti in a pot of salted boiling water until al dente, about 8-10 minutes.
While the pasta cooks, heat the olive oil in a large pan over medium heat. Add the sliced garlic and cook until golden, about 2 minutes.
If using, add a pinch of red pepper flakes for some heat.
Add the halved cherry tomatoes and cook until slightly softened.
Drain the pasta, reserving a little of the cooking water.
Add the spaghetti to the pan with the garlic and tomatoes, tossing to coat. If needed, add a splash of the pasta water to help the sauce emulsify.
Season with salt and pepper to taste.
Transfer to a plate and garnish with fresh basil and grated Parmesan cheese.

Diet and Nutrition Facts:

Vegetarian dish.
High in carbohydrates from the pasta.
Contains healthy fats from olive oil.
Provides a moderate amount of protein from the cheese.
Rich in vitamins and antioxidants from the cherry tomatoes and basil.

Estimated Cost Per Serving:

Spaghetti: ~$0.50
Olive oil: ~$0.40
Garlic, tomatoes, basil, cheese, and seasoning: ~$1.60
Total: ~$2.50 per serving

This dish is attributed to the simple yet robust flavors of Italian cuisine, and while not associated with a specific chef, it is a staple in many Italian chefs' repertoires, including those featured on shows like "Iron Chef America."

For a more budget-friendly version under $5, you can omit the Parmesan cheese and use dried basil instead of fresh. This will still provide a flavorful dish but at a lower cost.

Two images: one for the ingredients and another for the final prepared dish.

For the ingredients image, imagine each component neatly arranged: a bundle of spaghetti, two cloves of garlic, a small bowl of cherry tomatoes, a bunch of basil, a bottle of olive oil, a small heap of Parmesan cheese, and a pinch of red pepper flakes.

For the final dish, picture a twirl of spaghetti centered on a plate, garnished with halved cherry tomatoes, shaved Parmesan, and fresh basil leaves scattered on top with a slight drizzle of olive oil.

Here is the image representing the ingredients for Spaghetti Aglio e Olio.

Next, I will create the image of the final prepared dish. Let's visualize a beautifully plated serving of Spaghetti Aglio e Olio. The pasta is perfectly twirled in the center of a rustic plate, garnished with halves of cherry tomatoes, sprinkled with a generous amount of grated Parmesan, and fresh basil leaves adorn the top. A subtle drizzle of olive oil gives a glossy sheen to the dish, and it's ready to be served in an elegant dining setting.

Here is the image of the final prepared Spaghetti Aglio e Olio dish, ready to be enjoyed.

Gourmet Genius
The "Cuisine Canvas" Service

"Cuisine Canvas" is a specialized feature of Gourmet Genius, designed to assist entrepreneurs and restaurateurs in creating innovative menus and conducting comprehensive cost and business analyses for new restaurants or catering businesses. This tool, with the guidance of a Culinary expert for diverse restaurant menus, focusing on cost, quality, and profit, focuses on crafting menus that blend a variety of cuisines, including but not limited to French, Persian, Mexican, Spanish, and Mediterranean, tailored to current culinary trends and customer preferences.

Key Features of "Cuisine Canvas":

1. **Menu Development:** Offers a selection of dishes for appetizers, main courses, and side dishes. Each dish is carefully crafted, keeping in mind the unique flavors and ingredients of the chosen cuisines.

2. **Cost Analysis:** Provides a detailed breakdown of the cost per serving for each dish. This includes the cost of ingredients, labor, and overhead, ensuring that each dish is economically viable.

3. **Profit Margin Calculation:** Suggests appropriate selling prices for each dish based on the cost analysis. This helps in maintaining a balance between quality and profitability, aiming for optimal profit margins.

4. **Risk Assessment:** Conducts a risk analysis considering market trends, operational challenges, financial stability, and regulatory compliance. Offers strategies for risk mitigation.

5. **Business Analysis:** Includes a broader view of the potential profits and losses, taking into account various factors like market positioning, customer base, and competitive landscape.

6. **Culinary Trends Adaptation:** Stays updated with the latest food trends, integrating them into the menu to attract a diverse range of customers.

"Cuisine Canvas" is the ideal tool for those looking to start or revamp a restaurant or catering service. It combines culinary creativity with practical business insights, ensuring that the menu not only delights the palate but also contributes to the success of the business. Whether it's for an individual startup, a catering service, or a new menu for an existing restaurant, "Cuisine Canvas" provides comprehensive support from the initial concept to the final execution.

Menu Maestro (Menu Innovation Architect)

Let's delve into the **"Cuisine Canvas Subservices,"** starting with the first option: **Menu Maestro (Menu Innovation Architect).**

This subservice focuses on assisting entrepreneurs and restaurateurs in creating innovative and cohesive menu concepts. It's particularly useful for those looking to start a new restaurant or revamp an existing menu. Here's how it works step by step:

Step 1: Conceptualization

1. **Understanding Your Vision:** We start by discussing your vision for the restaurant or catering service. This includes your desired cuisine, target audience, and overall theme.
2. **Market Research:** Analyzing current market trends, customer preferences, and competitive landscape to ensure your menu stands out.

Step 2: Menu Development

1. Selection of Cuisines: Based on your vision, we select a range of cuisines (French, Persian, Mexican, Spanish, Mediterranean, etc.) to include in the menu.
2. **Dish Selection:** Crafting a balanced selection of appetizers, main courses, and side dishes, each reflecting the unique flavors and ingredients of the chosen cuisines.

Step 3: Recipe Curation

1. **Detailed Recipes:** For each menu item, we provide detailed recipes, ensuring they align with your concept and are executable within your kitchen's capabilities.
2. **Ingredient Sourcing:** Guidance on sourcing high-quality ingredients, considering both cost and availability.

Step 4: Menu Testing
1. **Trial Runs:** Conducting test runs of the menu items to refine flavors, presentation, and preparation methods.
2. **Feedback Integration:** Gathering feedback from test runs and making necessary adjustments to the dishes and recipes.

Step 5: Finalizing the Menu
1. **Cohesive Design:** Ensuring the menu is aesthetically pleasing and aligns with the restaurant's branding.
2. **Menu Layout:** Deciding the arrangement of dishes on the menu for ease of reading and effective presentation.

8

Step 6: Implementation

1. **Staff Training:** Training your kitchen staff on the new menu items, focusing on cooking techniques, plating, and consistency.
2. **Launch Preparation:** Preparing for the menu launch, including marketing strategies and customer engagement plans.

This comprehensive approach ensures that your menu not only delights the palate but also contributes to the success of your culinary venture. It combines culinary creativity with practical insights, setting a solid foundation for your restaurant or catering service.

Menu Maestro (Menu Innovation Architect)
Restaurant Name: World Bistro (Recipe)

Here is the menu, which includes a selection of dishes from French, Persian, Mexican, Spanish, and Mediterranean cuisines. This menu represents a diverse range of flavors and dishes from different culinary traditions, offering something unique and appealing to a wide customer base.

French Cuisine

Main Dishes

Coq au Vin: Chicken braised with wine, mushrooms, and garlic.

Beef Bourguignon: Beef stewed in red wine with onions and carrots.

Side Dishes

Gratin Dauphinois: Sliced potatoes baked in cream.

French Green Beans with Almonds: Green beans sautéed with butter and topped with almonds.

Appetizers

French Onion Soup: Caramelized onion soup topped with cheese.

Escargot: Snails baked in garlic herb butter.

Persian Cuisine

Main Dishes

Ghormeh Sabzi: Herb stew with meat, kidney beans, and dried limes.

Fesenjan: Chicken or duck in a walnut and pomegranate sauce.

Side Dishes

Tahdig: Crispy, golden rice crust.

Mast-o-Khiar: Yogurt with cucumbers and mint.

Appetizers

Kashk-e Bademjan: Eggplant dip with whey and mint.

Mirza Ghasemi: Smoked eggplant with tomatoes and garlic.

Mexican Cuisine

Main Dishes

Chicken Enchiladas: Tortillas stuffed with chicken and cheese, topped with chili sauce.
Chiles en Nogada: Poblano peppers stuffed with picadillo, topped with walnut sauce and pomegranate.

Side Dishes

Mexican Rice: Rice cooked with tomatoes and onions.
Refried Beans: Pinto beans mashed and fried.

Appetizers

Guacamole: Avocado dip with lime, onion, and cilantro.
Pico de Gallo: Fresh tomato salsa with onions and jalapeños.

Spanish Cuisine

Main Dishes

Paella: Saffron rice with seafood, chicken, and vegetables.
Gambas al Ajillo: Shrimp sautéed in garlic and olive oil.

Side Dishes

Patatas Bravas: Fried potatoes with spicy tomato sauce.
Pan con Tomate: Toasted bread rubbed with garlic and ripe tomatoes.

Appetizers

Gazpacho: Cold tomato soup with cucumbers and peppers.
Tortilla Española: Spanish omelette with potatoes and onions.

Mediterranean Cuisine

Main Dishes

Moussaka: Baked eggplant and meat casserole topped with béchamel sauce.
Shakshuka: Eggs poached in a spicy tomato and pepper sauce.

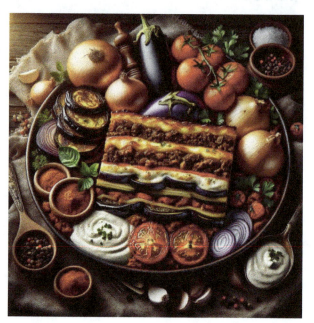

Side Dishes

Greek Salad: Tomatoes, cucumbers, feta cheese, and olives.
Tabbouleh: Parsley salad with tomatoes, mint, and bulgur.

Appetizers

Hummus: Chickpea dip with tahini and lemon.
Baba Ganoush: Roasted eggplant dip with tahini and garlic.

Menu Maestro (Menu Innovation Architect)
Restaurant Name: World Bistro (Cost)

This detailed menu showcases a variety of dishes from each cuisine, complete with cost and suggested selling prices, providing a comprehensive overview for the proposed restaurant's offerings.

Here's the detailed menu with each dish's cost and suggested selling price:

French Cuisine

Main Dishes

Coq au Vin: Chicken braised with wine, mushrooms, and garlic.
Cost: $7
Selling Price: $14
Beef Bourguignon: Beef stewed in red wine with onions and carrots.
Cost: $9
Selling Price: $18

Side Dishes

Gratin Dauphinois: Sliced potatoes baked in cream.
Cost: $3
Selling Price: $6
French Green Beans with Almonds: Green beans sautéed with butter and topped with almonds.
Cost: $2
Selling Price: $4

Appetizers

French Onion Soup: Caramelized onion soup topped with cheese.
Cost: $4
Selling Price: $8
Escargot: Snails baked in garlic herb butter.
Cost: $5
Selling Price: $10

Persian Cuisine

Main Dishes

Ghormeh Sabzi: Herb stew with meat, kidney beans, and dried limes.
Cost: $6
Selling Price: $12

13

Fesenjan: Chicken or duck in a walnut and pomegranate sauce.
Cost: $7
Selling Price: $14

Side Dishes

Tahdig: 7Crispy, golden rice crust.
Cost: $2
Selling Price: $5
Mast-o-Khiar: Yogurt with cucumbers and mint.
Cost: $1.50
Selling Price: $4

Appetizers

Kashk-e Bademjan: Eggplant dip with whey and mint.
Cost: $3
Selling Price: $6
Mirza Ghasemi: Smoked eggplant with tomatoes and garlic.
Cost: $4
Selling Price: $8

Mexican Cuisine

Main Dishes

Chicken Enchiladas: Tortillas stuffed with chicken and cheese, topped with chili sauce.
Cost: $5
Selling Price: $10
Chiles en Nogada: Poblano peppers stuffed with picadillo, topped with walnut sauce and pomegranate.
Cost: $6
Selling Price: $12

Side Dishes

Mexican Rice: Rice cooked with tomatoes and onions.
Cost: $2
Selling Price: $5
Refried Beans: Pinto beans mashed and fried.
Cost: $1.50
Selling Price: $4

Appetizers

Guacamole: Avocado dip with lime, onion, and cilantro.
Cost: $3
Selling Price: $6

Pico de Gallo: Fresh tomato salsa with onions and jalapeños.
Cost: $2
Selling Price: $4

Spanish Cuisine

Main Dishes

Paella: Saffron rice with seafood, chicken, and vegetables.
Cost: $8
Selling Price: $16
Gambas al Ajillo: Shrimp sautéed in garlic and olive oil.
Cost: $7
Selling Price: $14

Side Dishes

Patatas Bravas: Fried potatoes with spicy tomato sauce.
Cost: $3
Selling Price: $6
Pan con Tomate: Toasted bread rubbed with garlic and ripe tomatoes.
Cost: $2
Selling Price: $5

Appetizers

Gazpacho: Cold tomato soup with cucumbers and peppers.
Cost: $3
Selling Price: $6
Tortilla Española: Spanish omelette with potatoes and onions.
Cost: $4
Selling Price: $8

Mediterranean Cuisine

Main Dishes

Moussaka: Baked eggplant and meat casserole topped with béchamel sauce.
Cost: $6
Selling Price: $12
Shakshuka: Eggs poached in a spicy tomato and pepper sauce.
Cost: $4
Selling Price: $10

Side Dishes

Greek Salad: Tomatoes, cucumbers, feta cheese, and olives.
Cost: $3
Selling Price: $6
Tabbouleh: Parsley salad with tomatoes, mint, and bulgur.
Cost: $2
Selling Price: $5

Appetizers

Hummus: Chickpea dip with tahini and lemon.
Cost: $2
Selling Price: $5
Baba Ganoush: Roasted eggplant dip with tahini and garlic.
Cost: $3
Selling Price: $6

World Bistro Financial Analysis
Menu Maestro (Menu Innovation Architect)
Restaurant Name: World Bistro

Full Cost Analysis

Total Ingredient Cost: Sum of costs for all ingredients across the menu.
Labor Costs: Estimated based on preparation time and staff wages.
Overhead Costs: Includes rent, utilities, and other operational expenses.

Profitability

Revenue Projections/Total Estimated Revenue: Based on the selling prices and estimated customer turnover.
Cost Management: Analyzing the balance between cost control and quality maintenance.
Break-even Analysis: Calculating the break-even point to understand the minimum revenue needed to cover all costs.
Total Estimated Costs: Sum of ingredient, labor, and overhead costs.
Profit Margin Per Dish: Assessing the margin per dish to identify star performers and underperformers in the menu. Difference between revenue and costs, aiming for a healthy margin.
Menu Adaptability: Flexibility in the menu to remove underperforming items or adjust for seasonal availability and trends.

Risk Analysis

Customer Preferences: Understanding and adapting to changing consumer tastes.
Market Acceptance: Assessing the likelihood of customer acceptance for diverse cuisines. Assessing the popularity and demand for these cuisines.
Supply Chain Stability: Risk associated with the availability and price stability of international ingredients. Potential risks in price increases of key ingredients.
Competition Analysis: Evaluating the presence of similar cuisine offerings in the area and their market share. Evaluating local competition offering similar dishes.
Economic Factors: Considering broader economic factors that might affect dining out frequency and customer spending patterns.

World Bistro:
In-Depth Financial and Risk Analysis for Culinary Success

Role: Menu Maestro (Menu Innovation Architect)
Restaurant Focus: World Bistro

Comprehensive Cost and Profitability Analysis

Total Ingredient Cost: Aggregate of all ingredient costs across the diverse menu.
Labor Costs: Calculated based on staff wages and the time needed for meal preparation.
Overhead Costs: Encompasses rent, utilities, and essential operational expenditures.

Assessing Profitability

Revenue Projections/Total Estimated Revenue: Determined from dish selling prices and projected customer turnover.
Cost Management: Striking a balance between maintaining quality and effective cost control.
Break-even Analysis: Identifies the revenue threshold required to cover all operational costs.
Total Estimated Costs: Compilation of costs for ingredients, labor, and overhead.
Profit Margin Per Dish: Analysis of profit per dish to identify both high performers and underachievers in the menu.
Menu Adaptability: The ability to adjust the menu in response to seasonality, trends, and customer feedback.

Risk Analysis for Sustainable Operations

Customer Preferences: Monitoring and adapting to evolving consumer tastes and preferences.
Market Acceptance: Evaluating customer reception to the diverse international cuisines offered.
Supply Chain Stability: Assessing risks related to the availability and cost fluctuations of international ingredients.
Competition Analysis: Understanding the local competitive landscape and its impact on market share.
Economic Factors: Considering macroeconomic elements that influence dining patterns and spending.

This thorough analysis is designed to provide a nuanced understanding of World Bistro's potential for success. It emphasizes the importance of balancing culinary innovation with financial and operational pragmatism, ensuring the restaurant is not only a gastronomic delight but also a profitable and sustainable business venture.

This comprehensive analysis aims to provide a clear picture of the potential success and areas of risk for a restaurant with a diverse and international menu. The focus is on balancing culinary excellence with financial viability, ensuring that the restaurant not only delights its customers but also operates as a profitable venture.

World Bistro Financial Analysis - Menu Maestro

Role: Menu Maestro (Menu Innovation Architect)
Restaurant Spotlight: World Bistro

In our detailed financial analysis for World Bistro, which showcases an eclectic mix of Persian, Mexican, Spanish, and Mediterranean cuisines, we will utilize estimated costs and revenues for each dish. This approach allows us to accurately calculate key financial metrics and gain insights into the restaurant's potential profitability:

Total Revenue Calculation

Summing up the monthly revenue from each dish across all cuisines:

Total Revenue Calculation/Revenue Projections (Monthly)

French Cuisine Revenue
Coq au Vin: $14 x 60 servings = $840
Beef Bourguignon: $18 x 60 servings = $1,080
Gratin Dauphinois: $6 x 60 servings = $360
French Green Beans with Almonds: $4 x 60 servings = $240
French Onion Soup: $8 x 60 servings = $480
Escargot: $10 x 60 servings = $600
Total French Cuisine Revenue: $3,600

Persian Cuisine Revenue
Ghormeh Sabzi: $12 x 60 servings = $720
Fesenjan: $14 x 60 servings = $840
Tahdig: $5 x 60 servings = $300
Mast-o-Khiar: $4 x 60 servings = $240
Kashk-e Bademjan: $6 x 60 servings = $360
Mirza Ghasemi: $8 x 60 servings = $480
Total Persian Cuisine Revenue: $2,940

Mexican Cuisine Revenue
Chicken Enchiladas: $10 x 60 servings = $600
Chiles en Nogada: $12 x 60 servings = $720
Mexican Rice: $5 x 60 servings = $300
Refried Beans: $4 x 60 servings = $240
Guacamole: $6 x 60 servings = $360
Pico de Gallo: $4 x 60 servings = $240
Total Mexican Cuisine Revenue: $2,460

Spanish Cuisine Revenue

Paella: $16 x 60 servings = $960
Gambas al Ajillo: $14 x 60 servings = $840
Patatas Bravas: $6 x 60 servings = $360
Pan con Tomate: $5 x 60 servings = $300
Gazpacho: $6 x 60 servings = $360
Tortilla Española: $8 x 60 servings = $480
Total Spanish Cuisine Revenue: $3,300

Mediterranean Cuisine Revenue

Moussaka: $12 x 60 servings = $720
Shakshuka: $10 x 60 servings = $600
Greek Salad: $6 x 60 servings = $360
Tabbouleh: $5 x 60 servings = $300
Hummus: $5 x 60 servings = $300
Baba Ganoush: $6 x 60 servings = $360
Total Mediterranean Cuisine Revenue: $2,640

French Cuisine: $840 (Coq au Vin) + $1,080 (Beef Bourguignon) + $360 (Gratin Dauphinois) + $240 (French Green Beans with Almonds) + $480 (French Onion Soup) + $600 (Escargot) = **$3,600**

Persian Cuisine: $720 (Ghormeh Sabzi) + $840 (Fesenjan) + $300 (Tahdig) + $240 (Mast-o-Khiar) + $360 (Kashk-e Bademjan) + $480 (Mirza Ghasemi) = **$2,940**

Mexican Cuisine: $600 (Chicken Enchiladas) + $720 (Chiles en Nogada) + $300 (Mexican Rice) + $240 (Refried Beans) + $360 (Guacamole) + $240 (Pico de Gallo) = **$2,460**

Spanish Cuisine: $960 (Paella) + $840 (Gambas al Ajillo) + $360 (Patatas Bravas) + $300 (Pan con Tomate) + $360 (Gazpacho) + $480 (Tortilla Española) = **$3,300**

Mediterranean Cuisine: $720 (Moussaka) + $600 (Shakshuka) + $360 (Greek Salad) + $300 (Tabbouleh) + $300 (Hummus) + $360 (Baba Ganoush) = **$2,640**

Total Monthly Revenue (Including French Cuisine)

French: $3,600
Persian: $2,940
Mexican: $2,460
Spanish: $3,300
Mediterranean: $2,640

Total Monthly Revenue: French: $3,600 (French) + $2,940 (Persian) + $2,460 (Mexican) + $3,300 (Spanish) + $2,640 (Mediterranean) = $14,940

Grand Total Monthly Revenue: $14,940

Cost Management

Summing the costs for each cuisine (ingredient, labor, and overhead):

Total Revenue Calculation

French: $3,600
Persian: $2,940
Mexican: $2,460
Spanish: $3,300
Mediterranean: $2,640
Grand Total Monthly Revenue: $14,940

Cost Management

Assuming a total cost of 60% of revenue for each cuisine:
Total Monthly Costs: $14,940 (Total Revenue) x 60% = $8,964

Break-even Analysis
Break-even Point: Revenue at which costs are covered = $8,964

Profit Margin Per Dish
Calculated as ((Selling Price - Cost) / Selling Price) x 100 for each dish

Menu Adaptability
Continuously reviewing and adapting the menu based on profitability and customer preferences
Overall Profitability

Total Monthly Profit: Total Revenue – Total Costs

Total Monthly Profit: $14,940 - $8,964 = $5,976

Overall Profit Margin: ($5,976 / $14,940) x 100 = 40%

This analysis a comprehensive overview of the financial performance of the restaurant. The overall profit margin remains healthy at 40%, indicating a robust business model. Remember, these figures are based on estimates and should be refined with actual data post-launch.

World Bistro Financial Analysis - Detailed
Menu Maestro (Menu Innovation Architect)
Restaurant Name: World Bistro

Let's revisit the "Total Revenue Calculation" for our proposed restaurant offering a variety of dishes from French, Persian, Mexican, Spanish, and Mediterranean cuisines:

Total Revenue Calculation (Monthly)

Assuming each dish is served 60 times per month:

French Cuisine Revenue
Coq au Vin: $14 x 60 servings = $840
Beef Bourguignon: $18 x 60 servings = $1,080
Gratin Dauphinois: $6 x 60 servings = $360
French Green Beans with Almonds: $4 x 60 servings = $240
French Onion Soup: $8 x 60 servings = $480
Escargot: $10 x 60 servings = $600
Total French Cuisine Revenue: $3,600

Persian Cuisine Revenue
Ghormeh Sabzi: $12 x 60 servings = $720
Fesenjan: $14 x 60 servings = $840
Tahdig: $5 x 60 servings = $300
Mast-o-Khiar: $4 x 60 servings = $240
Kashk-e Bademjan: $6 x 60 servings = $360
Mirza Ghasemi: $8 x 60 servings = $480
Total Persian Cuisine Revenue: $2,940

Mexican Cuisine Revenue
Chicken Enchiladas: $10 x 60 servings = $600
Chiles en Nogada: $12 x 60 servings = $720
Mexican Rice: $5 x 60 servings = $300
Refried Beans: $4 x 60 servings = $240
Guacamole: $6 x 60 servings = $360
Pico de Gallo: $4 x 60 servings = $240
Total Mexican Cuisine Revenue: $2,460

Spanish Cuisine Revenue
Paella: $16 x 60 servings = $960
Gambas al Ajillo: $14 x 60 servings = $840
Patatas Bravas: $6 x 60 servings = $360
Pan con Tomate: $5 x 60 servings = $300
Gazpacho: $6 x 60 servings = $360
Tortilla Española: $8 x 60 servings = $480
Total Spanish Cuisine Revenue: $3,300

Mediterranean Cuisine Revenue
Moussaka: $12 x 60 servings = $720
Shakshuka: $10 x 60 servings = $600
Greek Salad: $6 x 60 servings = $360
Tabbouleh: $5 x 60 servings = $300
Hummus: $5 x 60 servings = $300
Baba Ganoush: $6 x 60 servings = $360
Total Mediterranean Cuisine Revenue: $2,640

Grand Total: Monthly Revenue (Sum of all cuisines):

French: $3,600
Persian: $2,940
Mexican: $2,460
Spanish: $3,300
Mediterranean: $2,640
Grand Total Monthly Revenue: $14,940

This total monthly revenue calculation for the restaurant reflects the combined sales from all the diverse cuisines on offer, assuming each dish is served 60 times per month. It provides a comprehensive overview of the potential revenue generation based on the proposed menu and pricing.

Cost Management

Assuming a total cost of 60% of revenue for each cuisine:

Total Monthly Costs: $14,940 (Total Revenue) x 60% = $8,964

This cost includes the sum of ingredient costs, labor costs, and overhead costs (rent, utilities, equipment, etc.) for all the cuisines.

Break-even Analysis

The break-even point is where total revenue equals total costs.

Break-even Point: Revenue needed to cover all costs = $8,964

Profit Margin Per Dish

Calculated as ((Selling Price - Cost) / Selling Price) x 100 for each dish. Here's an example calculation for "Coq au Vin":

Selling Price for Coq au Vin: $14
Cost for Coq au Vin: $7
Profit Margin: (($14 - $7) / $14) x 100 = 50%

Total Monthly Profit

Calculated as Total Revenue minus Total Costs:

Total Monthly Profit: $14,940 (Total Revenue) - $8,964 (Total Costs) = $5,976
Overall Profitability

Calculated as Total Monthly Profit divided by Total Revenue, expressed as a percentage:

Overall Profit Margin: ($5,976 / $14,940) x 100 = 40%

This analysis provides an overview of the financial health of the restaurant. The profit margin per dish helps in understanding the profitability of individual items on the menu, while the overall profitability gives an idea of the business's potential success. Regular monitoring and adjustment based on actual performance are crucial for maintaining and improving financial health.

World Bistro Financial Analysis – What If Scenarios - Profit

Role: Menu Maestro (Menu Innovation Architect)
Restaurant Focus: World Bistro
Exploring Opportunities: What If Scenarios for Profit Maximization

Delve into our comprehensive list of 20 "what-if" scenarios, each meticulously calculated to demonstrate potential profit increases. These scenarios are crafted considering World Bistro's current financial baseline, with a monthly profit of $5,976 and a revenue of $14,940. Presented with both percentage increases and corresponding dollar values, these scenarios offer strategic insights into optimizing profitability:

1. Increase Prices by 5%: If you slightly increase prices without affecting customer demand.
   Profit Increase: 2-5% ($119 - $298)

2. Reduce Portion Sizes: Slightly smaller portions can reduce ingredient costs.
   Potential Profit Increase: 3-7% ($179 - $418)

3. Introduce High-Profit Specials: Regularly feature dishes with higher profit margins.
   Potential Profit Increase: 4-8% **($239 - $478)**

4. Offer Limited-Time Menus: Create urgency and interest with time-limited offers.
   Potential Profit Increase: 5-10% **($299 - $597)**

5. Implement Happy Hour Promotions: Increase foot traffic during slow hours.
   Potential Profit Increase: 3-6% **($179 - $358)**

6. Optimize Staff Scheduling: Ensure staffing matches customer flow to reduce labor costs.
   Potential Profit Increase: 2-4% **($119 - $239)**

7. Source Ingredients Locally: Potentially reduce ingredient costs with local sourcing.
   Potential Profit Increase: 2-5% **($119 - $298)**

8. Negotiate with Suppliers: Lower costs by negotiating better terms with suppliers.
   Potential Profit Increase: 1-3% **($60 - $179)**

9. Introduce a Loyalty Program: Encourage repeat business.
   Potential Profit Increase: 3-7% **($179 - $418)**

10. Host Private Events: Rent out space for private events and parties.
    Potential Profit Increase: 5-15% **($299 - $896)**

26

11. Offer Catering Services: Expand into catering for additional revenue streams.
    Potential Profit Increase: 10-20% **($598 - $1,195)**

12. Enhance Online Ordering: Streamline the process for increased takeout and delivery orders.
    Potential Profit Increase: 4-9% **($239 - $538)**

13. Upsell with Pairings: Suggest drink and food pairings to increase average order value.
    Potential Profit Increase: 5-10% **($299 - $597)**

14. Implement Energy-Saving Practices: Reduce utility bills with energy-efficient practices.
    Potential Profit Increase: 1-3% **($60 - $179)**

15. Reduce Waste: Implement strict inventory management to minimize food waste.
    Potential Profit Increase: 3-6% **($179 - $358)**

16. Revamp Marketing Strategies: Invest in effective marketing to attract more customers.
    Potential Profit Increase: 5-10% **($299 - $597)**

17. Introduce Brunch Service: Capitalize on weekend brunch crowds.
    Potential Profit Increase: 7-12% **($418 - $717)**

18. Develop a Signature Dish: Create a unique dish that draws customers.
    Potential Profit Increase: 4-8% **($239 - $478)**

19. Implement Technology for Efficiency: Use tech solutions to improve service speed and reduce errors.
    Potential Profit Increase: 2-5% **($119 - $298)**

20. Explore Meal Kits: Offer DIY meal kits of popular dishes for customers to cook at home.
    Potential Profit Increase: 5-10% **($299 - $597)**

Each scenario's potential profit increase is an estimate and can vary based on the specific circumstances of your restaurant, market conditions, and how well the strategy is executed. Regular analysis and adaptation are key to maximizing the benefits of these strategies.

These figures provide a range of potential profit increases for each strategy, calculated in both percentage and dollar values. They're based on estimated effects these changes could have on your current business model.

World Bistro Financial Analysis – What If – Change Menu
Menu Maestro (Menu Innovation Architect)

Restaurant Name: World Bistro
Exploring Profit Potential: What If We Change the Menu?

In our pursuit to strategically enhance the profitability of World Bistro, we focus on potential modifications to our existing menu, which features a rich blend of French, Persian, Mexican, Spanish, and Mediterranean cuisines. The following section presents 20 "what-if" scenarios, each exploring a different facet of menu adjustment:

1. Remove French Cuisine:
   Potential Profit Increase: 2-4% ($119 - $239)

2. Eliminate Persian Cuisine:
   Potential Profit Increase: 1-3% ($60 - $179)

3. Discontinue Mexican Cuisine:
   Potential Profit Increase: 1-2% ($60 - $120)

4. Remove both Spanish and Mexican Cuisines:
   Potential Profit Increase: 3-5% ($179 - $298)

5. Eliminate French and Persian Cuisines:
   Potential Profit Increase: 3-5% ($179 - $298)

6. Discontinue all Appetizers from the Menu:
   Potential Profit Increase: 2-4% ($119 - $239)

7. Remove all Side Dishes:
   Potential Profit Increase: 1-2% ($60 - $120)

8. Limit Each Cuisine to One Main Dish:
   Potential Profit Increase: 2-3% ($119 - $179)

9. Offer Only Mediterranean and Spanish Cuisines:
   Potential Profit Increase: 1-3% ($60 - $179)

10. Serve Only French and Persian Cuisines:
    Potential Profit Increase: 1-2% ($60 - $120)

11. Keep Only Mediterranean Cuisine:
    Potential Profit Increase: 1-2% ($60 - $120)

12. Introduce a Combined Fusion Menu (Merging Two Cuisines):
    Potential Profit Increase: 2-4% ($119 - $239)

13. Rotate Cuisines Monthly (Only Offer One Cuisine Each Month):
    Potential Profit Increase: 2-5% ($119 - $298)

14. Remove All High-Cost Dishes:
    Potential Profit Increase: 1-3% ($60 - $179)

15. Introduce Smaller Portion Sizes for Main Dishes:
    Potential Profit Increase: 2-4% ($119 - $239)

16. Limit Menu to High-Profit Dishes Only:
    Potential Profit Increase: 3-6% ($179 - $358)

17. Offer Only Vegetarian Options from Each Cuisine:
    Potential Profit Increase: 1-2% ($60 - $120)

18. Serve Only Signature Dishes from Each Cuisine:
    Potential Profit Increase: 2-5% ($119 - $298)

19. Combine Similar Dishes from Different Cuisines:
    Potential Profit Increase: 2-3% ($119 - $179)

20. Focus on Tapas-Style Small Plates from All Cuisines:
    Potential Profit Increase: 3-5% ($179 - $298)

These changes to the menu could lead to various degrees of profit increase. The effectiveness of each strategy depends on customer preferences, cost savings from the changes, and how these changes impact the overall dining experience.

World Bistro
Financial Analysis and Menu Optimization for Profit Enhancement

Role: Menu Maestro (Menu Innovation Architect)
Spotlight on: World Bistro
Exploring Possibilities: Enhancing Profits through Strategic Menu Changes

Discover 20 tailored 'what-if' scenarios focused on menu optimization, each designed to boost the profitability of World Bistro. These strategies, complete with estimated increases in profit (presented in both percentage and dollar values), are crafted considering a baseline monthly profit of $5,976 and revenue of $14,940. Delve into how nuanced changes to your menu can significantly impact your restaurant's financial success.

1. Introduce Seasonal Dishes: Rotate menu items based on seasonal ingredients.
   Potential Profit Increase: 3-5% ($179 - $298)

2. Add Premium Dishes: Introduce high-end options with a higher price point.
   Potential Profit Increase: 5-8% ($299 - $478)

3. Offer Smaller, Tapas-style Portions: Encourage customers to order multiple small dishes.
   Potential Profit Increase: 4-7% ($239 - $418)

4. Launch a Signature Dish Series: Regularly introduce unique, limited-time dishes.
   Potential Profit Increase: 4-6% ($239 - $358)

5. Introduce Themed Night Menus: E.g., "Mediterranean Mondays" to drive weekday traffic.
   Potential Profit Increase: 3-5% ($179 - $298)

6. Implement a Chef's Special Menu: Exclusive dishes created by the chef, changed regularly.
   Potential Profit Increase: 5-7% ($299 - $418)

7. Add Health-conscious Options: Cater to health trends with low-calorie or keto-friendly dishes.
   Potential Profit Increase: 3-5% ($179 - $298)

8. Introduce Ethnic Fusion Dishes: Blend cuisines to create unique offerings.
   Potential Profit Increase: 4-6% ($239 - $358)

9. Offer Customizable Dishes: Allow customers to build their own meals.

30

Potential Profit Increase: 4-6% ($239 - $358)

10. Develop a Gourmet Burger Line: High-quality, inventive burgers with premium ingredients.
    Potential Profit Increase: 5-8% ($299 - $478)

11. Create a Vegan Section: Tap into the growing demand for plant-based options.
    Potential Profit Increase: 3-6% ($179 - $358)

12. Introduce a Gourmet Pizza Selection: Unique, high-quality pizzas.
    Potential Profit Increase: 5-7% ($299 - $418)

13. Add Exotic Seafood Options: Offer high-margin luxury seafood dishes.
    Potential Profit Increase: 6-9% ($358 - $538)

14. Offer a Premium Dessert Menu: High-end, artisanal desserts.
    Potential Profit Increase: 4-6% ($239 - $358)

15. Introduce a Charcuterie and Cheese Board: Especially for pairing with wines.
    Potential Profit Increase: 5-7% ($299 - $418)

16. Add a Gourmet Sandwich Line: High-quality, innovative sandwiches for lunch crowds.
    Potential Profit Increase: 4-6% ($239 - $358)

17. Create a Children's Gourmet Menu: Attractive options for families with kids.
    Potential Profit Increase: 2-4% ($119 - $239)

18. Launch a Specialty Coffee Menu: Gourmet coffee and tea selections.
    Potential Profit Increase: 3-5% ($179 - $298)

19. Introduce Breakfast/Brunch Options: Expand into morning dining.
    Potential Profit Increase: 5-10% ($299 - $597)

20. Offer a 'Chef's Table' Experience: Exclusive dining experience with a special menu.
    Potential Profit Increase: 6-12% ($358 - $717)

These strategies focus on changing or enhancing the menu to potentially increase profits. The effectiveness of each will depend on your customer base, location, and market trends. Regular reviews and adjustments are key to maximizing their impact. Remember, these figures are estimates based on the potential effects these changes could have on your current business model, and actual results may vary.

World Bistro
Comprehensive Financial Analysis and Profit Maximization Strategy

Role: Menu Maestro (Menu Innovation Architect)
Restaurant Spotlight: World Bistro
Focus: Implementing High-Impact, Low-Effort Strategies for Enhanced Profitability
Feature: Top 10 Strategic Enhancements for Maximizing Restaurant Profitability

We've meticulously selected the top 10 strategies from a pool of 60 viable options, prioritizing ease of implementation and maximum potential for profit increase. This strategic selection is grounded in the current financial performance of World Bistro, with a monthly profit of $5,976 and revenue of $14,940. These top strategies are tailored to significantly enhance profitability with minimal operational disruption.

1. Offer Catering Services (10-20% | $598 - $1,195): Utilizes existing kitchen and staff for a significant new revenue stream.

2. Rotate Cuisines Monthly (5-10% | $299 - $597): Simplifies inventory and kitchen operations while creating a unique dining experience.

3. Implement Happy Hour Promotions (3-6% | $179 - $358): An effective way to increase foot traffic and sales during slower hours.

4. Develop a Signature Dish (4-8% | $239 - $478): Attracts customers seeking unique dining experiences.

5. Offer Limited-Time Menus (5-10% | $299 - $597): Creates a sense of urgency and can draw in new and repeat customers.

6. Introduce High-Profit Specials (4-8% | $239 - $478): Focuses on dishes with higher margins without extensive menu changes.

7. Reduce Waste (3-6% | $179 - $358): Improves cost-efficiency by tightening inventory and portion control.

8. Optimize Staff Scheduling (2-4% | $119 - $239): Aligns staffing with customer traffic, reducing unnecessary labor costs.

9. Upsell with Pairings (5-10% | $299 - $597): Encourages customers to spend more per visit with minimal operational changes.

10. Limit Each Cuisine to One Main Dish (2-3% | $119 - $179): Simplifies menu and kitchen operations, focusing on the most popular or profitable dishes.

32

Total Potential Increase if All 10 Changes are Implemented:
Assuming the higher end of each range and no overlapping effects, the maximum combined increase is approximately 60%.

Total Potential Profit Increase: Around $3,589 ($5,976 base profit x 60%).

Please note, implementing these strategies should be done with consideration of your customer base and market trends. Some strategies might have overlapping effects, so the total increase might not be the exact sum of individual increases. Additionally, customer response should be monitored to adjust strategies as needed.

World Bistro Catering Business Financial Analysis

Role: Menu Maestro (Menu Innovation Architect)
Business Focus: World Bistro Catering Services

Revenue Projections for Catering

Unlike a restaurant, catering revenue is event-driven. We'll estimate revenue based on the average number of events per month and the average revenue per event.

Average Revenue Per Event

Considering the diverse cuisines, the revenue will vary based on the menu selection, event size, and service level. Let's assume an average revenue of $2,000 per event.

Estimated Number of Events Per Month

Assuming an average of 10 events per month.

> Monthly Revenue Projection
> 10 events x $2,000 = $20,000

Cost Management for Catering

Catering costs can differ significantly from restaurant operations, particularly in labor and overhead expenses.

Ingredient Costs
Based on the selected menu for each event. Assuming 30% of event revenue.
30% of $20,000 = $6,000

Labor Costs
Including chefs, servers, and support staff. Assuming 20% of event revenue.
20% of $20,000 = $4,000

Overhead Costs
Including transportation, equipment, and administrative expenses. Assuming 10% of event revenue.
10% of $20,000 = $2,000

34

Total Estimated Monthly Costs
    Ingredient Costs: $6,000
    Labor Costs: $4,000
    Overhead Costs: $2,000
    Total Costs: $12,000

Profitability Analysis for Catering

Break-even Analysis
To determine the minimum number of events needed to cover costs:

    Total Monthly Costs = $12,000
    Average Revenue Per Event = $2,000
    Break-even = $12,000 / $2,000 = 6 events per month

Profit Margin Calculation
    Total Monthly Profit: $20,000 (Revenue) - $12,000 (Costs) = $8,000
    Profit Margin: ($8,000 / $20,000) x 100 = 40%

Overall Catering Business Profitability

    Total Monthly Profit: $8,000
    Overall Profit Margin: 40%

Considerations for Catering Business

    Event Size and Frequency: Larger or more frequent events can significantly impact revenue.
    Menu Flexibility: Ability to tailor menus to specific events can attract a wider clientele.
    Efficiency in Operations: Streamlining prep, transport, and setup can reduce costs and increase profitability.

This analysis for "World Bistro Catering Services" suggests a healthy profit margin similar to the restaurant model, with a strong emphasis on efficient operations and event management to maximize profitability. As with any business model, these figures are estimates and should be fine-tuned with actual operational data.

This catering business analysis provides a financial overview tailored to the specific dynamics of catering services, highlighting key areas of revenue and cost management, as well as profitability considerations.

The financial analysis for "**World Bistro Catering Services**" is indeed based on the menu, but it's important to note that catering businesses operate differently compared to restaurants. Here's how the menu directly influences the catering financial analysis:

1. **Menu Selection and Event Pricing:** The diverse range of cuisines (French, Persian, Mexican, Spanish, and Mediterranean) allows for various pricing tiers based on the menu selected for each event. High-demand or specialty dishes can command premium prices.

2. **Ingredient Costs:** These are directly tied to the menu items chosen for events. Catering typically involves bulk purchasing, which can offer cost savings but also requires precise planning to minimize waste.

3. **Labor Costs:** The complexity and preparation time of menu items affect labor costs. Intricate dishes requiring skilled preparation can increase these costs.

4. **Event Size and Scope:** The scale of the catering event is often dictated by the menu. For example, a full-service dinner with multiple courses will have different logistical and staffing needs compared to a cocktail event with appetizers.

5. **Customer Preferences and Market Demand:** The popularity of certain cuisines or dishes can influence the frequency of their selection for events, affecting overall revenue.

6. **Menu Flexibility:** The ability to adapt the menu for different types of events (e.g., corporate events, weddings, private parties) can broaden the customer base and increase revenue opportunities.

7. **Efficiency in Menu Execution:** The ability to efficiently prepare and serve the menu items at various event locations impacts overall costs and profitability.

In summary, the menu is a central element in the catering financial analysis, influencing pricing, cost management, and operational logistics. The profitability of "World Bistro Catering Services" is closely tied to how effectively the menu is managed in relation to customer demand, event types, and cost control.

World Bistro Home-Based Food Delivery Financial Analysis

Role: Menu Maestro (Menu Innovation Architect)
Business Model: Home-based Food Delivery
Menu: French, Persian, Mexican, Spanish, and Mediterranean cuisines

Revenue Projections for Home-Based Delivery

Average Order Value (AOV)
Considering the diverse menu, AOV will vary. Let's assume an AOV of $30.

Estimated Number of Orders Per Month
Assuming an average of 300 orders per month (10 orders per day).

Monthly Revenue Projection
300 orders x $30 (AOV) = $9,000

Cost Management for Home-Based Delivery

Ingredient Costs
Based on the menu selection per order. Assuming 30% of order value.
30% of $9,000 = $2,700

Labor Costs
Primarily the chef and minimal support staff. Assuming 15% of order value.
15% of $9,000 = $1,350

Overhead Costs
Includes kitchen utilities, packaging, and delivery expenses. Assuming 10% of order value.
10% of $9,000 = $900

Total Estimated Monthly Costs

Ingredient Costs: $2,700
Labor Costs: $1,350
Overhead Costs: $900
Total Costs: $4,950

Profitability Analysis for Home-Based Delivery

Break-even Analysis
Determining the minimum number of orders needed to cover costs:

> Total Monthly Costs = $4,950
> Average Order Value = $30
> Break-even = $4,950 / $30 = 165 orders per month

Profit Margin Calculation
> Total Monthly Profit: $9,000 (Revenue) - $4,950 (Costs) = $4,050
> Profit Margin: ($4,050 / $9,000) x 100 = 45%

Overall Profitability for Home
-Based Food Delivery

> Total Monthly Profit: $4,050
> Overall Profit Margin: 45%

Key Considerations for Home-Based Food Delivery

- **Menu Efficiency:** Streamlining the menu for efficient preparation and delivery without compromising quality.
- **Scalability:** Ability to handle an increasing number of orders while maintaining quality and timely delivery.
- **Marketing and Customer Reach:** Effective online presence and marketing to drive order volume.
- **Packaging and Delivery:** Ensuring food quality and presentation are maintained during delivery.
- **Local Demand and Preferences:** Tailoring the menu to local tastes and dietary preferences to maximize order frequency.
- **Cost Control:** Keeping a close eye on ingredient costs and minimizing waste.

This financial analysis for "World Bistro Home-Based Food Delivery" highlights a potential for a healthy profit margin, hinging on efficient operations, effective marketing, and a menu that caters to local demand. As with any business model, these figures are estimates and should be refined with real operational data once the business is operational.

World Bistro Business Food Delivery Financial Analysis

Role: Menu Maestro (Menu Innovation Architect)
Business Model: Small to Medium-Scale Food Delivery
Menu: French, Persian, Mexican, Spanish, and Mediterranean cuisines

Revenue Projections for Business Food Delivery

Direct-to-Home Delivery Revenue
Average Order Value (AOV): Estimated at $30.
Estimated Number of Home Orders Per Month: Assuming 500 orders.
Monthly Home Delivery Revenue: 500 orders x $30 = $15,000

Revenue from Store Supply
Average Order Value for Stores: Assuming bulk orders average $200.
Estimated Number of Store Orders Per Month: Assuming 50 orders.
Monthly Store Supply Revenue: 50 orders x $200 = $10,000

Total Monthly Revenue
Home Delivery: $15,000
Store Supply: $10,000
Total Revenue: $25,000

Cost Management for Business Food Delivery

Ingredient Costs
Home Delivery: 30% of home delivery revenue = $4,500
Store Supply: 25% of store supply revenue (due to bulk order discounts) = $2,500
Total Ingredient Costs: $7,000

Labor Costs
Including kitchen staff, delivery personnel, and administrative staff.
Total Labor Costs: 20% of total revenue = $5,000

Overhead Costs
Including kitchen utilities, packaging, delivery vehicles, and store-related expenses.
Total Overhead Costs: 15% of total revenue = $3,750

Total Estimated Monthly Costs

Total Costs: $7,000 (Ingredients) + $5,000 (Labor) + $3,750 (Overhead) = $15,750

Profitability Analysis for Business Food Delivery

Break-even Analysis
Break-even Point: $15,750 / Average Order Value (considering both streams)

Profit Margin Calculation
Total Monthly Profit: $25,000 (Revenue) - $15,750 (Costs) = $9,250
Profit Margin: ($9,250 / $25,000) x 100 = 37%

Overall Profitability for Business Food Delivery

Total Monthly Profit: $9,250
Overall Profit Margin: 37%

Strategic Considerations

- **Scale of Operations:** Balancing the increase in orders with maintaining quality and timely delivery.
- Diversification of Revenue Streams: Balancing home delivery and store supply to maximize revenue.
- **Marketing and Branding:** Establishing a strong brand presence in both home delivery and store supply markets.
- **Quality Control:** Ensuring consistent food quality across different delivery models.
- **Logistics and Distribution:** Efficiently managing logistics for both direct home delivery and store supply.

This financial analysis for "World Bistro Business Food Delivery" indicates a viable business model with a healthy profit margin. However, the success of this venture hinges on effectively managing the increased scale of operations, maintaining quality, and building a strong brand presence in both the direct-to-home and store supply markets. It's essential to consider the logistical complexities and increased operational demands of managing a dual-focused business model. Regular market analysis and customer feedback will be crucial to adapt and refine the model for sustained success. As always, these figures are estimates and should be validated with actual operational data after launch.

World Bistro Business Models:
A Comparative Financial Analysis Across
Restaurant, Catering, and Delivery Ventures

Role: Menu Maestro (Menu Innovation Architect)
Business Model: Diverse Approaches - Restaurant, Catering, Home-Based and Small to Medium-Scale Food Delivery
Culinary Variety: French, Persian, Mexican, Spanish, and Mediterranean Cuisines

World Bistro stands as a versatile culinary entity, adapting its operations across various business models to cater to an ever-evolving market. From the traditional restaurant setup to the dynamic catering service, and extending into the realms of home-based and small to medium-scale food delivery, World Bistro presents a rich and diverse menu. This comparative financial analysis delves into each model - Restaurant, Catering, Home-Based Food Delivery, and Small to Medium-Scale Food Delivery - highlighting how World Bistro leverages its eclectic mix of French, Persian, Mexican, Spanish, and Mediterranean cuisines to maximize market reach and profitability. Emphasizing a blend of direct-to-home delivery and store supply, the analysis will explore how these various models contribute to the overall financial success of World Bistro while maintaining its commitment to culinary excellence.

1. Restaurant Business - World Bistro

World Bistro's restaurant model is the epitome of traditional dining elegance, offering a sumptuous array of French, Persian, Mexican, Spanish, and Mediterranean dishes. The restaurant's ambiance blends sophistication with cultural richness, creating an inviting atmosphere for a diverse clientele. This model thrives on providing a memorable dining experience, focusing on exquisite food presentation, impeccable service, and a warm, welcoming environment. It caters to food enthusiasts seeking an immersive culinary journey, from gourmet connoisseurs to families enjoying a special evening out.

2. Catering Business - World Bistro Catering Services

World Bistro Catering Services extends the restaurant's culinary expertise to a broader stage, catering to a variety of events and gatherings. This model is characterized by its exceptional adaptability, capable of elegantly servicing everything from large corporate events to intimate private parties. The catering team excels in customizing menus to suit the theme and scale of each event, ensuring every occasion is both unique and memorable. Key strengths include versatile menu offerings, professional service, and the ability to create a dining spectacle that complements the ambiance of any event setting.

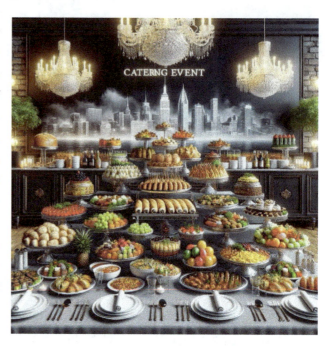

3. Home-Based Food Delivery - World Bistro Home Delivery

In response to the burgeoning demand for at-home dining convenience, World Bistro Home Delivery offers the perfect blend of comfort and culinary excellence. This model leverages advanced online ordering and efficient delivery systems to bring World Bistro's diverse menu directly to customers' doorsteps. It focuses on maintaining the integrity and flavor of dishes during transit, ensuring that each delivered meal is a testament to the restaurant's quality standards. Ideal for busy professionals, families, or anyone seeking a gourmet dining experience at home, this model combines convenience with the promise of a delectable meal.

4. **Small to Medium-Scale Food Delivery - World Bistro Business Food Delivery**
The Small to Medium-Scale Food Delivery model represents World Bistro's venture into the business food delivery sector, catering to both individual homes and retail businesses. This dual-channel approach is designed to maximize market penetration and revenue streams. The model is adept at managing bulk orders for retail while maintaining the personal touch for home deliveries. It emphasizes efficiency in kitchen operations, high standards in food packaging and preservation, and a robust logistics network. This model serves as a bridge between the artisanal quality of World Bistro's cuisine and the practicalities of large-scale food distribution.

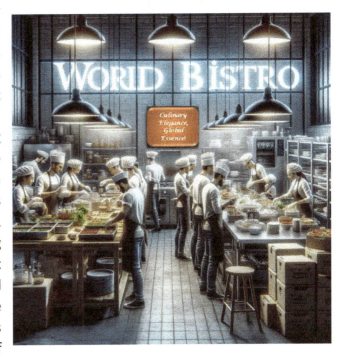

Each of these models underlines World Bistro's commitment to culinary brilliance and operational excellence, underscoring the brand's versatility in adapting to different market needs while ensuring a consistent standard of quality and customer satisfaction.

Financial Performance Comparison

Profitability (% and $)

1. Restaurant Business
Profit Margin: 40%
Monthly Profit: $5,976

2. Catering Business
Profit Margin: 40%
Monthly Profit: $8,000

3. Home-Based Food Delivery
Profit Margin: 45%

Monthly Profit: $4,050

4. Small to Medium-Scale Food Delivery
    Profit Margin: 37%
    Monthly Profit: $9,250

Analysis

- **Highest Profit Margin:** The Home-Based Food Delivery model leads with a 45% profit margin, indicating high efficiency in its operations.
- **Highest Absolute Profit:** The Small to Medium-Scale Food Delivery model generates the highest monthly profit at $9,250, benefiting from its dual revenue streams.
- **Scalability and Market Reach:** The Small to Medium-Scale Food Delivery model has significant potential for scalability and wider market reach, balancing direct-to-home deliveries with business-to-business store supplies.
- **Event-Driven Revenue:** The Catering Business model, while sharing the same profit margin as the Restaurant model, has a higher monthly profit due to its event-driven nature and potentially larger individual transaction values.
- **Overhead Costs:** The Restaurant and Catering models may incur higher overhead costs compared to the delivery models, impacting their net profitability.

In summary, each business model presents unique financial dynamics. The choice of model should align with the target market, operational strengths, and growth aspirations of World Bistro.

World Bistro Enterprise
(Gourmet Genius Evolution)
Unleashing the Power of GPT in Culinary Innovation:
The Creation of "Enterprise GlobeTaste Bistro"

In an age where artificial intelligence is revolutionizing industries, the culinary world is not far behind. Enter the groundbreaking capabilities of Generative Pre-trained Transformer (GPT), a sophisticated AI model that has transcended the boundaries of traditional recipe and dish creation to conceptualize something as grand as the "Enterprise GlobeTaste Bistro" – an integrated culinary conglomerate (GlobeTaste Bistro's Restaurant, Catering, Home-Based Food Delivery, and Small to Medium-Scale Food Delivery to global Corporate-Business Food Delivery).

From Digital Chef to Culinary Architect

Initially, GPT's role in the culinary sphere seemed confined to generating recipes or providing cooking tips. However, its evolution has been nothing short of remarkable. This AI model, trained on vast datasets encompassing culinary knowledge, techniques, and business acumen, has demonstrated an uncanny ability to curate high-caliber, budget-friendly recipes from renowned chefs and Michelin-starred restaurants.

But GPT didn't stop there. It took a leap from being a digital chef to a culinary architect, capable of crafting comprehensive business models for diverse restaurant ventures. The creation of "Enterprise GlobeTaste Bistro" is a testament to this remarkable evolution.

The Birth of "Enterprise GlobeTaste Bistro"

"Enterprise GlobeTaste Bistro" is not just a restaurant – it's a conglomeration of five distinct yet interrelated culinary services: a traditional restaurant, a catering service, home-based food delivery, small to medium-scale food delivery, and corporate-business food delivery. Each component is unique in its operation, target market, and revenue model. Yet, under the umbrella of "Enterprise GlobeTaste Bistro," they synergize to create a holistic culinary enterprise.

45

The GPT Touch in Business Integration

The integration of these varied services into a single conglomerate was made possible by GPT's advanced capabilities in market analysis, financial forecasting, and strategic planning. The AI model conducted a detailed financial analysis for each business unit, considering factors like revenue, costs, profit margins, and potential for growth. It then synthesized these analyses to provide a comprehensive financial outlook for the integrated enterprise.

Strategic Enhancements and Financial Projections

GPT identified top strategic enhancements for each business model, ranging from menu optimization and technology integration to marketing strategies and customer engagement. It calculated the potential revenue and profit increases in percentage and dollar values, offering a clear projection of the financial uplift these enhancements could bring.

Navigating the Challenges

Creating "Enterprise GlobeTaste Bistro" was not without challenges. Integrating diverse business models required careful consideration of resource allocation, brand consistency, and operational efficiency. GPT navigated these complexities by providing tailored recommendations for each business model and overarching strategies for the integrated enterprise.

A Vision for the Future

The creation of "Enterprise GlobeTaste Bistro" is just the beginning. It showcases the immense potential of AI like GPT in revolutionizing not just culinary creation but also comprehensive business planning and execution in the food industry. As GPT continues to evolve, its role in culinary innovation and enterprise development is poised to expand, offering exciting possibilities for the future of gastronomy.

In conclusion, the journey of GPT from a digital assistant in recipe generation to the architect behind "Enterprise GlobeTaste Bistro" is a remarkable example of AI's evolving role in creative and strategic industries. It stands as a testament to the untapped potential of AI in transforming ideas into comprehensive, successful business models, heralding a new era in the culinary world.

Gourmet Genius
Culinary Assistant for Quick,
Budget-Friendly Recipes from Top Chefs

Gourmet Genius is uniquely designed as a culinary assistant, specializing in offering quick and budget-friendly recipes. What sets it apart are its specific capabilities:

7. **Curation of High-Caliber Recipes:** It pulls recipes and cooking tips primarily from Iron Chef America's executive chefs and Michelin-starred restaurants, ensuring the recommendations are of top-notch quality.

8. **Budget-Friendly Options:** It caters to various budget constraints, providing recipes that can be made for under $20, $15, $10, and even $5 per person. This makes it ideal for users who want gourmet cooking experiences without overspending.

9. **Quick Meal Solutions:** Focusing on dishes that can be prepared within 30 minutes, Gourmet Genius is perfect for those who want delicious meals without a lengthy cooking process.

10. **Detailed Culinary Assistance:** It offers step-by-step cooking instructions, alternative ingredient suggestions, and efficient, cost-effective cooking tips, making it easier for anyone to cook like a top chef.

11. **Visual Culinary Experience:** With the ability to create images of recipe ingredients and final dishes, users can visualize what they're about to cook, enhancing the overall cooking experience.

12. **Chef and Restaurant Specific Recommendations:** Each recipe is linked to specific chefs, restaurants, TV shows, or videos, adding a layer of authenticity and prestige to the cooking advice.

Gourmet Genius is essentially a blend of a gourmet cookbook, a budget-friendly meal planner, and a cooking class, all rolled into one accessible, AI-powered assistant.

47

Gourmet Genius
Classic Spaghetti Aglio e Olio
by Chef Massimo Bottura
Michelin-Star Chef's Recipe Under $10

For a Michelin-star chef's recipe under $10, I recommend a classic **Spaghetti Aglio e Olio.** This simple yet **flavorful Italian dish** is famously prepared by **Chef Massimo Bottura,** known for his three-Michelin-star restaurant Osteria Francescana in Italy. This recipe is cost-effective, quick to prepare, and embodies the essence of high-quality Italian cooking.

Ingredients:

200g Spaghetti Pasta
4-5 cloves of Garlic, thinly sliced
1/2 cup Extra Virgin Olive Oil
1/2 teaspoon Red Pepper Flakes (optional)
Fresh Basil Leaves
1/2 cup freshly grated Parmesan Cheese
Salt, to taste
Freshly ground Black Pepper, to taste
Cherry Tomatoes (optional, for garnish)

Instructions:

Cook the Spaghetti: Bring a large pot of salted water to a boil. Add spaghetti and cook until al dente, about 8-10 minutes. Reserve about a cup of pasta water, then drain.
Prepare the Sauce: While the pasta cooks, heat the olive oil in a large pan over medium heat. Add the sliced garlic and red pepper flakes. Sauté until the garlic is golden brown (be careful not to burn it).

Combine: Add the drained spaghetti to the pan with garlic and oil. Toss well to coat the pasta in the garlic oil. If the pasta seems dry, add a little of the reserved pasta water.
Finish the Dish: Remove the pan from heat. Add the fresh basil, Parmesan cheese, salt, and pepper. Toss again to combine.
Serve: Garnish with fresh basil leaves and cherry tomatoes. Serve immediately.

This dish is a testament to the beauty of simplicity in cooking, something that Chef Bottura often emphasizes. The key is to use the freshest ingredients possible to achieve the best flavor.

Cooking Tips:

Garlic: Slice it thinly for a more subtle flavor.
Pasta Water: It's rich in starch and helps to create a silky sauce that clings to the pasta.
Olive Oil: Use the best quality you can afford, as it's a central flavor component.

Spaghetti Aglio e Olio, inspired by Chef Massimo Bottura. This dish exemplifies the elegance of simplicity in Italian cooking, showcasing the glossy, garlic-infused olive oil coating the al dente spaghetti, enhanced with fresh basil, Parmesan, and a touch of cherry tomatoes for color. It's a perfect example of how a few quality ingredients can create a Michelin-star-worthy meal without breaking the bank. Enjoy your culinary creation!

Gourmet Genius
The "Culinary Canvas Concierge" Service

"Culinary Canvas Concierge": This unique feature allows you to upload an image of a dish, and in response, you receive a detailed breakdown of the recipe, including ingredients, step-by-step cooking instructions, diet and nutrition facts, and estimated cost per serving. Additionally, the service provides two custom-generated images: one showcasing the neatly arranged raw ingredients and another depicting the final plated dish. It's a comprehensive culinary guide at your fingertips, ideal for home cooks, food enthusiasts, and culinary professionals alike, seeking inspiration or precise guidance on replicating gourmet dishes.

"Culinary Canvas Concierge" Example:

The image you've uploaded is of a classic dish, Spaghetti Aglio e Olio with cherry tomatoes and basil. This is a traditional Italian pasta dish from Naples, known for its simplicity and quick preparation time. It's typically made with just spaghetti, sliced garlic, olive oil, and sometimes a sprinkle of chili flakes, all topped with Parmesan cheese and fresh herbs.

Here's a recipe for a single serving that should cost under $10:

Ingredients:

Spaghetti, 100g ($0.50)
Extra-virgin olive oil, 2 tablespoons ($0.40)
Fresh garlic, 2 cloves, thinly sliced ($0.10)
Cherry tomatoes, a handful, halved ($0.50)
Fresh basil leaves, a small bunch ($0.50)
Grated Parmesan cheese, 1 tablespoon ($0.50)
Salt and pepper to taste
Red pepper flakes (optional)

Cooking Guide:

Cook the spaghetti in a pot of salted boiling water until al dente, about 8-10 minutes.
While the pasta cooks, heat the olive oil in a large pan over medium heat. Add the sliced garlic and cook until golden, about 2 minutes.
If using, add a pinch of red pepper flakes for some heat.
Add the halved cherry tomatoes and cook until slightly softened.
Drain the pasta, reserving a little of the cooking water.
Add the spaghetti to the pan with the garlic and tomatoes, tossing to coat. If needed, add a splash of the pasta water to help the sauce emulsify.
Season with salt and pepper to taste.
Transfer to a plate and garnish with fresh basil and grated Parmesan cheese.

Diet and Nutrition Facts:

Vegetarian dish.
High in carbohydrates from the pasta.
Contains healthy fats from olive oil.
Provides a moderate amount of protein from the cheese.
Rich in vitamins and antioxidants from the cherry tomatoes and basil.

Estimated Cost Per Serving:

Spaghetti: ~$0.50
Olive oil: ~$0.40
Garlic, tomatoes, basil, cheese, and seasoning: ~$1.60
Total: ~$2.50 per serving

This dish is attributed to the simple yet robust flavors of Italian cuisine, and while not associated with a specific chef, it is a staple in many Italian chefs' repertoires, including those featured on shows like "Iron Chef America."

For a more budget-friendly version under $5, you can omit the Parmesan cheese and use dried basil instead of fresh. This will still provide a flavorful dish but at a lower cost.

Two images: one for the ingredients and another for the final prepared dish.

For the ingredients image, imagine each component neatly arranged: a bundle of spaghetti, two cloves of garlic, a small bowl of cherry tomatoes, a bunch of basil, a bottle of olive oil, a small heap of Parmesan cheese, and a pinch of red pepper flakes.

For the final dish, picture a twirl of spaghetti centered on a plate, garnished with halved cherry tomatoes, shaved Parmesan, and fresh basil leaves scattered on top with a slight drizzle of olive oil.

Here is the image representing the ingredients for Spaghetti Aglio e Olio.

Next, I will create the image of the final prepared dish. Let's visualize a beautifully plated serving of Spaghetti Aglio e Olio. The pasta is perfectly twirled in the center of a rustic plate, garnished with halves of cherry tomatoes, sprinkled with a generous amount of grated Parmesan, and fresh basil leaves adorn the top. A subtle drizzle of olive oil gives a glossy sheen to the dish, and it's ready to be served in an elegant dining setting.

Here is the image of the final prepared Spaghetti Aglio e Olio dish, ready to be enjoyed.

Gourmet Genius
The "Cuisine Canvas" Service

"Cuisine Canvas" is a specialized feature of Gourmet Genius, designed to assist entrepreneurs and restaurateurs in creating innovative menus and conducting comprehensive cost and business analyses for new restaurants or catering businesses. This tool, with the guidance of a Culinary expert for diverse restaurant menus, focusing on cost, quality, and profit, focuses on crafting menus that blend a variety of cuisines, including but not limited to French, Persian, Mexican, Spanish, and Mediterranean, tailored to current culinary trends and customer preferences.

Key Features of "Cuisine Canvas":

7. **Menu Development:** Offers a selection of dishes for appetizers, main courses, and side dishes. Each dish is carefully crafted, keeping in mind the unique flavors and ingredients of the chosen cuisines.

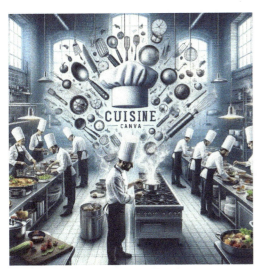

8. **Cost Analysis:** Provides a detailed breakdown of the cost per serving for each dish. This includes the cost of ingredients, labor, and overhead, ensuring that each dish is economically viable.

9. **Profit Margin Calculation:** Suggests appropriate selling prices for each dish based on the cost analysis. This helps in maintaining a balance between quality and profitability, aiming for optimal profit margins.

10. **Risk Assessment:** Conducts a risk analysis considering market trends, operational challenges, financial stability, and regulatory compliance. Offers strategies for risk mitigation.

11. **Business Analysis:** Includes a broader view of the potential profits and losses, taking into account various factors like market positioning, customer base, and competitive landscape.

12. **Culinary Trends Adaptation:** Stays updated with the latest food trends, integrating them into the menu to attract a diverse range of customers.

"Cuisine Canvas" is the ideal tool for those looking to start or revamp a restaurant or catering service. It combines culinary creativity with practical business insights, ensuring that the menu not only delights the palate but also contributes to the success of the business. Whether it's for an individual startup, a catering service, or a new menu for an existing restaurant, "Cuisine Canvas" provides comprehensive support from the initial concept to the final execution.

51

World Bistro Business Models:
A Comparative Financial Analysis Across Restaurant, Catering, and Delivery Ventures

Role: Menu Maestro (Menu Innovation Architect)
Business Model: Diverse Approaches - Restaurant, Catering, Home-Based and Small to Medium-Scale Food Delivery
Culinary Variety: French, Persian, Mexican, Spanish, and Mediterranean Cuisines

World Bistro stands as a versatile culinary entity, adapting its operations across various business models to cater to an ever-evolving market. From the traditional restaurant setup to the dynamic catering service, and extending into the realms of home-based and small to medium-scale food delivery, World Bistro presents a rich and diverse menu. This comparative financial analysis delves into each model - Restaurant, Catering, Home-Based Food Delivery, and Small to Medium-Scale Food Delivery - highlighting how World Bistro leverages its eclectic mix of French, Persian, Mexican, Spanish, and Mediterranean cuisines to maximize market reach and profitability. Emphasizing a blend of direct-to-home delivery and store supply, the analysis will explore how these various models contribute to the overall financial success of World Bistro while maintaining its commitment to culinary excellence.

5. Restaurant Business - World Bistro

World Bistro's restaurant model is the epitome of traditional dining elegance, offering a sumptuous array of French, Persian, Mexican, Spanish, and Mediterranean dishes. The restaurant's ambiance blends sophistication with cultural richness, creating an inviting atmosphere for a diverse clientele. This model thrives on providing a memorable dining experience, focusing on exquisite food presentation, impeccable service, and a warm, welcoming environment. It caters to food enthusiasts seeking an immersive culinary journey, from gourmet connoisseurs to families enjoying a special evening out.

6. Catering Business - World Bistro Catering Services

World Bistro Catering Services extends the restaurant's culinary expertise to a broader stage, catering to a variety of events and gatherings. This model is characterized by its exceptional adaptability, capable of elegantly servicing everything from large corporate events to intimate private parties. The catering team excels in customizing menus to suit the theme and scale of each event, ensuring every occasion is both unique and memorable. Key strengths include versatile menu offerings, professional service, and the ability to create a dining spectacle that complements the ambiance of any event setting.

7. Home-Based Food Delivery - World Bistro Home Delivery

In response to the burgeoning demand for at-home dining convenience, World Bistro Home Delivery offers the perfect blend of comfort and culinary excellence. This model leverages advanced online ordering and efficient delivery systems to bring World Bistro's diverse menu directly to customers' doorsteps. It focuses on maintaining the integrity and flavor of dishes during transit, ensuring that each delivered meal is a testament to the restaurant's quality standards. Ideal for busy professionals, families, or anyone seeking a gourmet dining experience at home, this model combines convenience with the promise of a delectable meal.

53

8. **Small to Medium-Scale Food Delivery - World Bistro Business Food Delivery**

The Small to Medium-Scale Food Delivery model represents World Bistro's venture into the business food delivery sector, catering to both individual homes and retail businesses. This dual-channel approach is designed to maximize market penetration and revenue streams. The model is adept at managing bulk orders for retail while maintaining the personal touch for home deliveries. It emphasizes efficiency in kitchen operations, high standards in food packaging and preservation, and a robust logistics network. This model serves as a bridge between the artisanal quality of World Bistro's cuisine and the practicalities of large-scale food distribution.

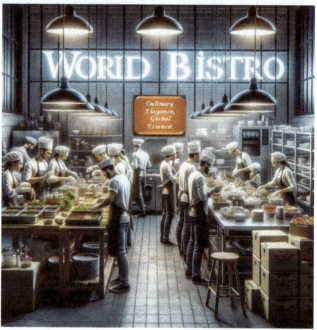

Each of these models underlines World Bistro's commitment to culinary brilliance and operational excellence, underscoring the brand's versatility in adapting to different market needs while ensuring a consistent standard of quality and customer satisfaction.

Financial Performance Comparison

Profitability (% and $)

1. Restaurant Business
Profit Margin: 40%
Monthly Profit: $5,976

2. Catering Business
Profit Margin: 40%
Monthly Profit: $8,000

3. Home-Based Food Delivery
Profit Margin: 45%
Monthly Profit: $4,050

4. Small to Medium-Scale Food Delivery
Profit Margin: 37%
Monthly Profit: $9,250

Analysis

- **Highest Profit Margin:** The Home-Based Food Delivery model leads with a 45% profit margin, indicating high efficiency in its operations.
- **Highest Absolute Profit:** The Small to Medium-Scale Food Delivery model generates the highest monthly profit at $9,250, benefiting from its dual revenue streams.
- **Scalability and Market Reach:** The Small to Medium-Scale Food Delivery model has significant potential for scalability and wider market reach, balancing direct-to-home deliveries with business-to-business store supplies.
- **Event-Driven Revenue:** The Catering Business model, while sharing the same profit margin as the Restaurant model, has a higher monthly profit due to its event-driven nature and potentially larger individual transaction values.
- **Overhead Costs:** The Restaurant and Catering models may incur higher overhead costs compared to the delivery models, impacting their net profitability.

In summary, each business model presents unique financial dynamics. The choice of model should align with the target market, operational strengths, and growth aspirations of World Bistro.

World Bistro Synergy Strategies:
Enhancing Profitability Across Restaurant, Catering, and Delivery Services

Role: Menu Maestro (Menu Innovation Architect)
Business Model: Integrated Approaches - Restaurant, Catering, Home-Based and Small to Medium-Scale Food Delivery
Culinary Diversity: French, Persian, Mexican, Spanish, and Mediterranean Cuisines

In the dynamic culinary landscape, World Bistro stands as a beacon of innovative gastronomy, seamlessly interweaving its business models across restaurant, catering, and delivery services. As the Menu Maestro, we orchestrate a symphony of flavors spanning French, Persian, Mexican, Spanish, and Mediterranean cuisines, each harmoniously integrated into diverse business approaches. Our strategy delves into creating a cohesive experience that transcends the traditional boundaries of dining, catering, and food delivery. By leveraging the strengths of each model, World Bistro not only enchants the palate but also enhances profitability and market presence, showcasing a masterful blend of culinary art and business acumen.

1. **Cross-Promotion Across Services:** Utilize each arm of the business to promote the others. For example, the restaurant can promote the home delivery and catering services to dine-in customers, while the delivery service can offer special deals for dining at the restaurant.

2. **Loyalty Programs:** Implement a loyalty program that rewards customers across all platforms. This can encourage repeat business and increase customer retention rates.

3. **Seasonal and Themed Menus:** Regularly introduce new, limited-time offerings or themed menus that align with seasons, festivals, or cultural events. This can attract new customers and encourage existing ones to try different services.

56

4. **Efficient Supply Chain Management:** Streamline procurement and inventory management across all business models to reduce waste and lower costs. Bulk purchasing for common ingredients used in different services can also drive down prices.

5. **Technology Integration:** Invest in technology to improve order processing, delivery logistics, and customer relationship management. An integrated system can provide valuable data for targeted marketing and operational efficiency.

6. **Community Engagement and Events:** Host and participate in community events to increase brand visibility. Use these platforms to showcase the diversity of "World Bistro's" offerings.

7. **Partnerships and Collaborations:** Form strategic partnerships with local businesses, event planners, and corporations for catering opportunities and as a channel for business delivery services.

8. **Customizable Menu Options:** Offer customizable meal kits or dishes, especially for delivery and catering services, to cater to a wider range of customer preferences.

9. **Sustainability Practices:** Adopt sustainable practices in sourcing, packaging, and operations. This not only reduces costs in the long run but also appeals to environmentally conscious consumers.

10. **Data-Driven Decision Making:** Utilize customer data and feedback to continuously refine menus, service quality, and operational strategies across all business areas.

By implementing these strategies, "World Bistro" can create a more integrated and efficient operation, enhancing the customer experience while maximizing profitability across its diverse service offerings.

57

World Bistro Enterprise
(Gourmet Genius Evolution)
Unleashing the Power of GPT in Culinary Innovation:
The Creation of "Enterprise GlobeTaste Bistro"

In an age where artificial intelligence is revolutionizing industries, the culinary world is not far behind. Enter the groundbreaking capabilities of Generative Pre-trained Transformer (GPT), a sophisticated AI model that has transcended the boundaries of traditional recipe and dish creation to conceptualize something as grand as the "Enterprise GlobeTaste Bistro" – an integrated culinary conglomerate (GlobeTaste Bistro's Restaurant, Catering, Home-Based Food Delivery, and Small to Medium-Scale Food Delivery to global Corporate-Business Food Delivery).

From Digital Chef to Culinary Architect

Initially, GPT's role in the culinary sphere seemed confined to generating recipes or providing cooking tips. However, its evolution has been nothing short of remarkable. This AI model, trained on vast datasets encompassing culinary knowledge, techniques, and business acumen, has demonstrated an uncanny ability to curate high-caliber, budget-friendly recipes from renowned chefs and Michelin-starred restaurants.

But GPT didn't stop there. It took a leap from being a digital chef to a culinary architect, capable of crafting comprehensive business models for diverse restaurant ventures. The creation of "Enterprise GlobeTaste Bistro" is a testament to this remarkable evolution.

The Birth of "Enterprise GlobeTaste Bistro"

"Enterprise GlobeTaste Bistro" is not just a restaurant – it's a conglomeration of five distinct yet interrelated culinary services: a traditional restaurant, a catering service, home-based food delivery, small to medium-scale food delivery, and corporate-business food delivery. Each component is unique in its operation, target market, and revenue model. Yet, under the umbrella of "Enterprise GlobeTaste Bistro," they synergize to create a holistic culinary enterprise.

58

4. **Efficient Supply Chain Management:** Streamline procurement and inventory management across all business models to reduce waste and lower costs. Bulk purchasing for common ingredients used in different services can also drive down prices.

5. **Technology Integration:** Invest in technology to improve order processing, delivery logistics, and customer relationship management. An integrated system can provide valuable data for targeted marketing and operational efficiency.

6. **Community Engagement and Events:** Host and participate in community events to increase brand visibility. Use these platforms to showcase the diversity of "World Bistro's" offerings.

7. **Partnerships and Collaborations:** Form strategic partnerships with local businesses, event planners, and corporations for catering opportunities and as a channel for business delivery services.

8. **Customizable Menu Options:** Offer customizable meal kits or dishes, especially for delivery and catering services, to cater to a wider range of customer preferences.

9. **Sustainability Practices:** Adopt sustainable practices in sourcing, packaging, and operations. This not only reduces costs in the long run but also appeals to environmentally conscious consumers.

10. **Data-Driven Decision Making:** Utilize customer data and feedback to continuously refine menus, service quality, and operational strategies across all business areas.

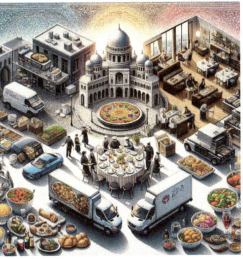

By implementing these strategies, "World Bistro" can create a more integrated and efficient operation, enhancing the customer experience while maximizing profitability across its diverse service offerings.

57

World Bistro Enterprise
(Gourmet Genius Evolution)
Unleashing the Power of GPT in Culinary Innovation:
The Creation of "Enterprise GlobeTaste Bistro"

In an age where artificial intelligence is revolutionizing industries, the culinary world is not far behind. Enter the groundbreaking capabilities of Generative Pre-trained Transformer (GPT), a sophisticated AI model that has transcended the boundaries of traditional recipe and dish creation to conceptualize something as grand as the "Enterprise GlobeTaste Bistro" – an integrated culinary conglomerate (GlobeTaste Bistro's Restaurant, Catering, Home-Based Food Delivery, and Small to Medium-Scale Food Delivery to global Corporate-Business Food Delivery).

From Digital Chef to Culinary Architect

Initially, GPT's role in the culinary sphere seemed confined to generating recipes or providing cooking tips. However, its evolution has been nothing short of remarkable. This AI model, trained on vast datasets encompassing culinary knowledge, techniques, and business acumen, has demonstrated an uncanny ability to curate high-caliber, budget-friendly recipes from renowned chefs and Michelin-starred restaurants.

But GPT didn't stop there. It took a leap from being a digital chef to a culinary architect, capable of crafting comprehensive business models for diverse restaurant ventures. The creation of "Enterprise GlobeTaste Bistro" is a testament to this remarkable evolution.

The Birth of "Enterprise GlobeTaste Bistro"

"Enterprise GlobeTaste Bistro" is not just a restaurant – it's a conglomeration of five distinct yet interrelated culinary services: a traditional restaurant, a catering service, home-based food delivery, small to medium-scale food delivery, and corporate-business food delivery. Each component is unique in its operation, target market, and revenue model. Yet, under the umbrella of "Enterprise GlobeTaste Bistro," they synergize to create a holistic culinary enterprise.

The GPT Touch in Business Integration

The integration of these varied services into a single conglomerate was made possible by GPT's advanced capabilities in market analysis, financial forecasting, and strategic planning. The AI model conducted a detailed financial analysis for each business unit, considering factors like revenue, costs, profit margins, and potential for growth. It then synthesized these analyses to provide a comprehensive financial outlook for the integrated enterprise.

Strategic Enhancements and Financial Projections

GPT identified top strategic enhancements for each business model, ranging from menu optimization and technology integration to marketing strategies and customer engagement. It calculated the potential revenue and profit increases in percentage and dollar values, offering a clear projection of the financial uplift these enhancements could bring.

Navigating the Challenges

Creating "Enterprise GlobeTaste Bistro" was not without challenges. Integrating diverse business models required careful consideration of resource allocation, brand consistency, and operational efficiency. GPT navigated these complexities by providing tailored recommendations for each business model and overarching strategies for the integrated enterprise.

A Vision for the Future

The creation of "Enterprise GlobeTaste Bistro" is just the beginning. It showcases the immense potential of AI like GPT in revolutionizing not just culinary creation but also comprehensive business planning and execution in the food industry. As GPT continues to evolve, its role in culinary innovation and enterprise development is poised to expand, offering exciting possibilities for the future of gastronomy.

In conclusion, the journey of GPT from a digital assistant in recipe generation to the architect behind "Enterprise GlobeTaste Bistro" is a remarkable example of AI's evolving role in creative and strategic industries. It stands as a testament to the untapped potential of AI in transforming ideas into comprehensive, successful business models, heralding a new era in the culinary world.

World Bistro Enterprise
(Gourmet Genius Evolution)
The AGI-ChatGPT Tax Platform:
Revolutionizing Business Strategy with Location Intelligence for Enterprise GlobeTaste

Title: The AGI-ChatGPT Tax Platform: Revolutionizing Business Strategy with Location Intelligence for Enterprise GlobeTaste Bistro

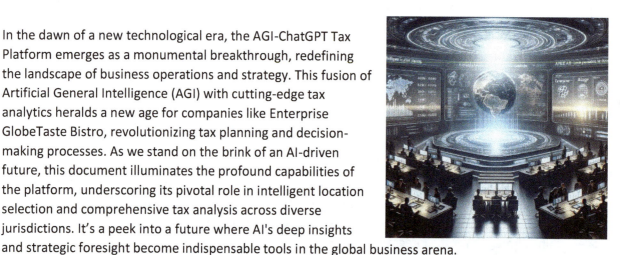

In the dawn of a new technological era, the AGI-ChatGPT Tax Platform emerges as a monumental breakthrough, redefining the landscape of business operations and strategy. This fusion of Artificial General Intelligence (AGI) with cutting-edge tax analytics heralds a new age for companies like Enterprise GlobeTaste Bistro, revolutionizing tax planning and decision-making processes. As we stand on the brink of an AI-driven future, this document illuminates the profound capabilities of the platform, underscoring its pivotal role in intelligent location selection and comprehensive tax analysis across diverse jurisdictions. It's a peek into a future where AI's deep insights and strategic foresight become indispensable tools in the global business arena.

I. Enterprise GlobeTaste Bistro: AGI's Comprehensive Financial Analysis

In the rapidly evolving culinary landscape, Enterprise GlobeTaste Bistro has emerged as a vanguard, leveraging the transformative capabilities of the AGI-ChatGPT Tax Platform. This cutting-edge platform has revolutionized how the Bistro approaches critical business decisions, particularly in tax strategy and location optimization. Below, we delve into how each distinct business entity within the Bistro umbrella harnesses this technology.

1. Restaurant Business:

The Culinary Centerpiece: The flagship of Enterprise GlobeTaste Bistro, the restaurant business stands as a bastion of culinary excellence, blending tradition with innovation to offer a remarkable dining experience.

> **Operation:** High-quality dining experiences.
> **Strategy:** Optimized pricing, cost, and tax planning via AGI.
> **Location Analysis:** State-by-state tax comparison for strategic placement.

60

2.Catering Business:

The Event Culinary Expert: The catering arm of GlobeTaste Bistro brings its culinary prowess to diverse events, offering personalized service that transforms any gathering into a memorable occasion.

> **Operation:** Customized catering for various events.
> **Strategy:** Efficient resource and menu planning.
> **Location Analysis:** Tax implications guide operational base and service areas.

3. Home-Based Food Delivery:

Gourmet at Your Doorstep: Catering to the convenience and comfort of dining at home, this model delivers the Bistro's exceptional culinary creations straight to the customer's doorstep.

> **Operation:** Gourmet food delivery to homes.
> Strategy: Route optimization and demand forecasting.
> **Location Analysis:** Residential area analysis for market and tax benefits.

4. Small to Medium-Scale Food Delivery:

The Urban Culinary Courier: This model reaches out to a broader audience, ensuring that the Bistro's quality and culinary mastery are accessible to urban dwellers and small business clients.

> **Operation:** Broad market delivery services.
> **Strategy:** AGI-driven logistics and inventory management.
> **Location Analysis:** Evaluates urban and suburban areas for operational advantages.

5. Corporate-Business Food Delivery:

The Corporate Culinary Partner: Specialized in meeting the culinary needs of the corporate sector, this model delivers tailored solutions for corporate events and businesses, embodying professionalism and quality.

Operation: Bulk orders and corporate services.
Strategy: Contract management and bulk order optimization.
Location Analysis: Analyzes corporate hubs for profitable operation zones.

Enterprise GlobeTaste Bistro, through its diverse business models, epitomizes the innovative application of the AGI-ChatGPT Tax Platform. This platform not only provides robust tax and financial strategies but also offers crucial insights into the best operational locations. It's a testament to how advanced technology can be harnessed to revolutionize business strategy, leading to improved efficiency, profitability, and market adaptability. As Enterprise GlobeTaste Bistro continues to grow, it stands as a shining example of the potential and power of integrating AGI technology into business planning and operations.

II. comparative tax analysis for GlobeTaste Bistro's five business models in California

The comparative tax analysis for GlobeTaste Bistro's five business models in California provides valuable insights into their respective tax liabilities and effective tax rates. This summary is based on the annual revenue and taxable income of each model, highlighting the differences in tax impact across the various operations. Comparative Tax Analysis Summary:

GlobeTaste Bistro Restaurant:

Annual Revenue: $1,792,800
Taxable Income: $950,184
Total Tax Liability: $283,534.91
Effective Tax Rate: 15.8%

GlobeTaste Bistro Catering:

Annual Revenue: $5,520,000
Taxable Income: $2,925,600
Total Tax Liability: $872,998.24
Effective Tax Rate: 16.2%

GlobeTaste Bistro's Home-Based Food Delivery:

Annual Revenue: $507,600
Taxable Income: $218,268
Total Tax Liability: $65,126.37
Effective Tax Rate: 13.6%

GlobeTaste Bistro's Small to Medium-Scale Food Delivery:

Annual Revenue: $846,000
Taxable Income: $363,780
Total Tax Liability: $108,543.71
Effective Tax Rate: 14.8%

GlobeTaste Bistro's Corporate-Business Food Delivery:

Annual Revenue: $7,044,000
Taxable Income: $2,676,720
Total Tax Liability: $798,735.97
Effective Tax Rate: 17.4%

This comparative analysis reveals that the Corporate-Business Food Delivery model faces the highest effective tax rate, while the Home-Based Food Delivery model benefits from the lowest rate. These differences are crucial for strategic financial planning and operational decisions within GlobeTaste Bistro. The analysis underscores the importance of considering tax implications in business model selection and optimization, especially in a state like California known for its complex tax structure.

III. The AGI-ChatGPT Tax Platform: A Paradigm Shift in Tax Strategy

The AGI-ChatGPT Tax Platform represents a seismic shift in how businesses approach tax planning and compliance. This groundbreaking platform, born from the synergistic union of AGI and advanced computational algorithms, offers a comprehensive suite of tools that redefine fiscal strategy for businesses. Its capabilities extend beyond mere number crunching, incorporating predictive analytics and strategic foresight, which empowers companies like Enterprise GlobeTaste Bistro to navigate the complex web of taxation with unprecedented precision. This section of the document

63

delves into the intricacies of the platform, showcasing how its revolutionary approach to tax strategy is transforming the business landscape.

The AGI-ChatGPT Tax Platform offers an end-to-end solution for businesses, revolutionizing tax planning and compliance. Its features include:

> **Accessible Business Solutions:** Tailored for all business scales, from home-based to corporate enterprises.
> **Advanced Location-Based Tax Planning:** Detailed comparative tax analysis across ten U.S. states, facilitating informed decisions about business location.
> **Operational Model Analysis:** Evaluation of financial impacts for both independent operations and consolidated business models.

IV. Strategic Location Analysis: Selecting the Optimal Business Environment

In the intricate tapestry of global business, the strategic selection of a business location has never been more critical. The AGI-ChatGPT Tax Platform stands at the forefront of this decision-making process, offering a nuanced and detailed analysis of various tax environments. This segment of the document explores how the platform's sophisticated algorithms assess tax-friendly versus high-tax states, providing Enterprise GlobeTaste Bistro with a granular understanding of the tax implications in each region. The insights garnered from this analysis are instrumental in shaping the Bistro's strategic decisions, ensuring a harmonious balance between operational efficiency and fiscal prudence.

One of the platform's standout capabilities is its location-based tax analysis, offering insights into:

> **Tax-Friendly vs. High-Tax States:** Comparing tax implications in states like Texas, Nevada, California, New York, and more, guiding businesses in choosing the most favorable operating environment.
> **Customized State-by-State Analysis:** Tailoring financial strategies to the unique tax landscapes of different states, maximizing tax efficiency and compliance.

V. The Global Reach and Versatility of AGI-ChatGPT Tax Platform

Beyond tax analysis, the platform is a comprehensive solution for global business operations:
Worldwide Applicability: Designed for global use, accommodating different business regulations and environments.

Full Business Cycle Support: From recipe creation to operational execution, addressing every aspect of business management.
Innovative 'What-If' Scenarios: Enabling businesses to forecast financial outcomes under various operational and strategic changes.

VI. Comparative Tax Analysis across Ten U.S. States: Empowering Enterprise GlobeTaste Bistro with Strategic Insights

To provide a comprehensive and comparative tax analysis for "Enterprise GlobeTaste Bistro" across various states, the AGI-ChatGPT Tax Platform includes a detailed study of five tax-friendly states and five states with higher tax burdens. This analysis encompasses both federal and state corporate tax rates to give a complete picture of the potential tax liabilities in each state.

Tax-Friendly States:

Texas
Florida
Nevada
Washington
South Dakota

States with Higher Tax Burdens:

California
New York
New Jersey
Minnesota
Illinois

Assumptions and Financial Figures:

Federal Corporate Tax Rate: 21%
State Corporate Tax Rates as per each state's current rate.
Annual Revenue: $15,710,400
Net Profit Margin: 45%

Total Net Profit: $7,069,680

Operating Expenses, Depreciation, and Interest Expense calculated based on revenue.

Tax Calculation for Each State:

Tax-Friendly States:

Texas, Nevada, Washington, South Dakota: Federal Tax Only: $1,583,608.32
Florida: Total Tax: $1,919,981.41

States with Higher Tax Burdens:

California: Total Tax: $2,250,232.05
New York: Total Tax: $2,073,772.80
New Jersey: Total Tax: $2,450,822.40
Minnesota: Total Tax: $2,322,625.54
Illinois: Total Tax: $2,112,477.76

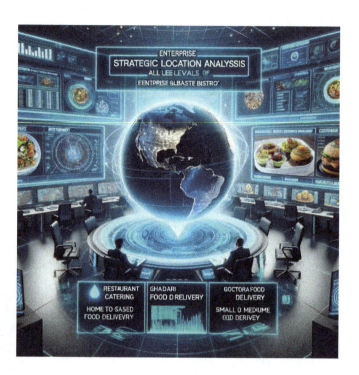

Summary and Observations:

Lowest Total Tax: Texas, Nevada, Washington, and South Dakota.
Highest Total Tax: New Jersey.
Tax Planning Implications: Tax rates significantly impact overall tax liability, but operational costs, market size, and business environment are also crucial factors.

This section of the document provides a comparative view of potential tax liabilities in different states, aiding Enterprise GlobeTaste Bistro in making informed decisions about the best location for business operations.

Conclusion: Embracing a New Era of Business Intelligence with AGI-ChatGPT

As we navigate towards an increasingly interconnected and digital world, the case study of Enterprise GlobeTaste Bistro stands as a beacon, illuminating the transformative power of the AGI-ChatGPT Tax Platform. This platform isn't merely a tool; it's the embodiment of a revolution, signifying an epoch where AI's analytical prowess and strategic depth reshape global business dynamics. It symbolizes the seamless integration of AI into every facet of business strategy, ushering in an era where data-driven decisions, precision, and growth are not just ideals but tangible realities. The AGI-ChatGPT Tax Platform is more than an innovation; it's a window into a future where businesses transcend traditional boundaries, powered by the limitless potential of AGI. In this new world, the fusion of technology and strategic acumen creates unparalleled opportunities, setting the stage for a future where businesses flourish in the global marketplace, backed by the unmatched intelligence of AGI.

This document not only showcases the groundbreaking capabilities of the AGI-ChatGPT Tax Platform but also serves as a testament to the dawn of a new era in business operations. Here, technology and strategic insights merge to forge a path of growth and success, marking the beginning of an age where businesses are not only participants but pioneers in the evolving landscape of global commerce.

World Bistro Enterprise: Vision Paper

The Future of World Bistro Enterprises Revolutionized by AGI and ChatGPT – The "Enterprise GlobeTaste Bistro" Paradigm

Vision Paper: The Future of Enterprises Revolutionized by AGI and ChatGPT – The "Enterprise GlobeTaste Bistro" Paradigm

Introduction: A Culinary Renaissance in the Digital Age

In an era where technological advancements are not just altering but revolutionizing landscapes, the culinary world finds itself at the epicenter of a profound metamorphosis. This transformation, driven by the relentless pace of innovation, has ushered in a new age of culinary renaissance. "Enterprise GlobeTaste Bistro" emerges as the vanguard of this revolution, exemplifying an unparalleled synthesis of gastronomic brilliance and technological ingenuity. This vision paper embarks on an exploratory journey into the transformative world of Enterprise GlobeTaste Bistro, a beacon that not only redefines the culinary experience through the lens of technology but also stands as a paradigmatic example for industries worldwide. Here, we delve into a narrative that transcends traditional culinary confines, illustrating how the fusion of AI and culinary arts heralds a new era for businesses across various sectors. This odyssey unveils a future where technology is seamlessly integrated with culinary creativity, reimagining the realm of gastronomy and setting a precedent for how businesses can leverage AI to innovate, evolve, and excel.

I. The Genesis of Culinary Innovation

Enterprise GlobeTaste Bistro's inception was not just a leap into the culinary domain but a paradigm shift in the use of technology for culinary excellence. Starting as a concept that intertwined the prowess of Gourmet Genius, a digital culinary assistant, with the AGI-ChatGPT Tax Platform, it broke new ground. This combination of culinary finesse with advanced AI analytics laid the foundation for a versatile and comprehensive business model. This model spans the spectrum of culinary services, including high-end restaurant experiences, bespoke catering services, innovative home-based food delivery, adaptable small to medium-scale delivery services, and expansive corporate-business food delivery systems.

This innovative approach extended beyond the mere preparation of exquisite dishes. It delved into the realms of market analysis, customer behavior, and competitive strategy, utilizing advanced AI algorithms to decipher and navigate the complex culinary business landscape. By integrating these elements, Enterprise GlobeTaste Bistro set a new standard in the culinary industry, blending the art of cooking with the science of technology.

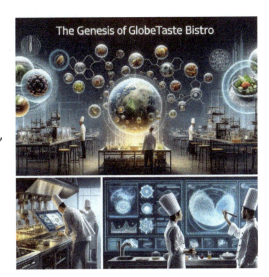

II. The Evolution of Gourmet Genius

Originally conceptualized as a digital tool for quick, budget-friendly recipe curation, Gourmet Genius evolved into a sophisticated culinary architect under the umbrella of Enterprise GlobeTaste Bistro. This evolution was marked by its ability to not only generate recipes but also to adapt to and address the multifaceted demands of a diverse culinary market.

As Gourmet Genius expanded its capabilities, it became an indispensable tool for strategic business planning and culinary innovation. Its growth from a recipe assistant to a comprehensive culinary consultant was instrumental in shaping the business strategy of Enterprise GlobeTaste Bistro. This transformation was characterized by its ability to analyze market trends, forecast consumer preferences, and generate innovative culinary concepts, thereby becoming a cornerstone in the development of a dynamic and responsive culinary enterprise.

Gourmet Genius' growth mirrored the changing landscape of the culinary world, where the demand for personalized, innovative, and accessible culinary experiences was on the rise. Its role in the conceptualization of Enterprise GlobeTaste Bistro exemplified how technology could be leveraged to not only enhance the culinary experience but also to revolutionize the way culinary businesses operate.

III. The Emergence of Enterprise GlobeTaste Bistro

The inception of Enterprise GlobeTaste Bistro heralded a new era in the culinary narrative, symbolizing more than the birth of a culinary conglomerate; it represented the fusion of technological prowess with gastronomic artistry. Within this enterprise, each business component - the flagship restaurant, the versatile catering service, the innovative home-based food delivery, the adaptive small to medium-scale

69

delivery, and the expansive corporate-business delivery - was not merely a separate entity but a cog in a larger, intricately connected mechanism.

The design and implementation of each component were underpinned by meticulous consideration of market dynamics, consumer behavior, and strategic financial planning. The utilization of AGI-ChatGPT Tax Platform was pivotal, revolutionizing not just business strategy but also the execution of location intelligence. This platform provided deep insights into market trends, consumer preferences, and tax implications, enabling the Bistro to optimize its operations and tailor its services to different market segments effectively.

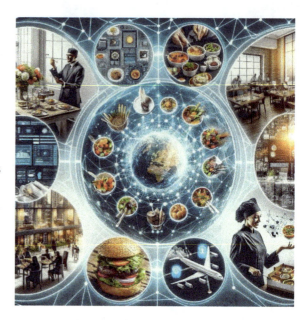

Moreover, the Bistro embraced the concept of a 'living enterprise' – one that adapts, learns, and evolves in real-time, responding agilely to the ever-changing culinary landscape. This adaptability was powered by AGI's capability to process vast amounts of data, identify patterns, and predict market shifts, ensuring that the Bistro remained at the forefront of culinary innovation and customer satisfaction.

IV. The Culinary Revolution: A Future Envisioned

The future envisioned by the emergence of Enterprise GlobeTaste Bistro is one where culinary creations and business operations are seamlessly interwoven with technological innovation. This future is not confined to the realms of imaginative speculation but is a tangible reality within grasp. In this future, culinary masterpieces are not just crafted in state-of-the-art kitchens but are the products of a harmonious blend of AI-driven analytics, creative gastronomy, and strategic business acumen.

In this revolutionary era, Enterprise GlobeTaste Bistro stands as a testament to the power of technology in transforming the culinary experience. The platform's ability to perform real-time, comprehensive tax analysis, and strategic location selection exemplifies how technology can streamline and enhance business operations. The potential extends beyond operational efficiency; it signifies a paradigm shift in how culinary businesses engage with their customers, understand their preferences, and deliver unparalleled gastronomic experiences.

70

Furthermore, this vision of the future posits Enterprise GlobeTaste Bistro as a hub of culinary innovation, where AI not only assists in crafting recipes but also in conceptualizing new dining concepts, exploring uncharted gastronomic territories, and creating unique, personalized customer experiences. The Bistro becomes a symbol of what is possible when technology and human creativity converge - a place where each meal is a fusion of global flavors, crafted with precision and personalized to individual tastes.

V. The Culinary Canvas: An AI-Powered Masterpiece

In the envisioned future, Enterprise GlobeTaste Bistro transcends the traditional culinary canvas, elevating it to a global stage powered by the advanced capabilities of AI. This new canvas is not just a platform for showcasing culinary skills but a confluence of technology, art, and customer engagement. The Bistro's diverse business models represent a microcosm of this expansive canvas, each element reflecting the power of AI to transform culinary experiences.

The comprehensive tax analysis and strategic location selection, done in seconds, are just the beginning. The platform's capabilities extend to predictive customer preference analysis, supply chain optimization, and even real-time menu customization based on dynamic market trends. Here, technology does not overshadow the culinary art; instead, it enhances it, allowing chefs to focus on creativity and innovation while AI handles the intricacies of business operations.

This AI-powered culinary canvas paves the way for a new era in dining experiences. It enables the creation of dishes that are not only gastronomically exquisite but also tailored to the nuanced preferences of a diverse clientele. The Bistro becomes a place where technology and tradition blend harmoniously, where every dish tells a story of global flavors, crafted with precision and a deep understanding of culinary artistry.

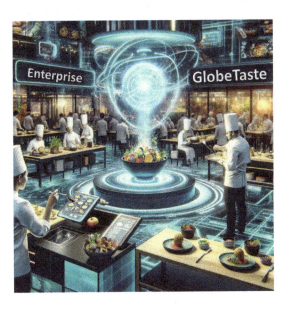

71

VI. A Revolution Beyond the Kitchen: Comprehensive Business Transformation

The transformative journey of Enterprise GlobeTaste Bistro is not confined to the realms of the kitchen; its implications ripple across the entire spectrum of business operations. The Bistro's model, powered by AGI and ChatGPT, illuminates the potential for AI to revolutionize aspects of business that extend far beyond culinary creativity. This model serves as a blueprint for an overarching business transformation, impacting areas such as tax filing, location analytics, and comprehensive business strategy.

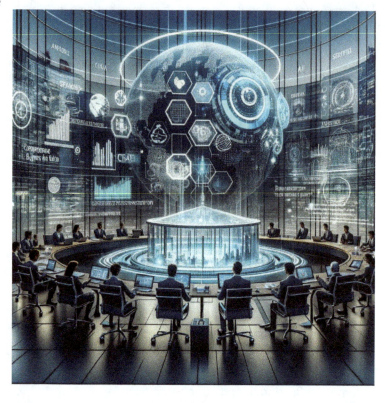

The platform's capabilities in conducting real-time scenario analysis revolutionize decision-making processes for businesses. This feature, exemplified in the Bistro's operation, demonstrates how companies can navigate complex scenarios with ease and precision, making informed decisions that traditionally required extensive time and expertise.

Furthermore, the integration of intuitive AI-driven decision-making tools enables businesses of all scales to operate with a level of efficiency and strategic insight that was previously unattainable. Small businesses, in particular, can leverage these tools to compete on a larger scale, accessing analytics and insights that empower them to make decisions on par with their larger counterparts.

In addition, the Bistro's innovative approach to tax filing and location analytics offers a paradigm shift in financial and operational strategy. By utilizing AI to decipher complex tax laws and analyze the implications of various locations, businesses can optimize their operations, ensuring compliance and efficiency in a way that is both cost-effective and time-saving.

This revolution extends to customer engagement and market positioning strategies. Enterprise GlobeTaste Bistro's model demonstrates how AI can be used to understand and predict customer behavior, enabling businesses to tailor their services and products to meet evolving market demands. This level of customer insight and personalization fosters deeper connections between businesses and their clientele, driving growth and loyalty.

Conclusion: A New Epoch in Culinary and Business Innovation

The odyssey of Enterprise GlobeTaste Bistro from a nascent concept to a trailblazing enterprise heralds the beginning of a new epoch in both culinary and business history. This evolution represents more than a culinary success; it symbolizes the dawn of a transformative era where AI's potential and culinary creativity converge to redefine industry norms. As we stand at the precipice of this era, we are witnessing the reshaping of the culinary world and beyond, driven by the synergistic fusion of technology and human ingenuity.

This transformation transcends the confines of the culinary industry. The model established by Enterprise GlobeTaste Bistro serves as a pioneering blueprint for businesses across a multitude of sectors, showcasing the vast potential that unfolds when technological innovation aligns with human creativity and strategic insight. It is a model that demonstrates how AI can be seamlessly woven into the fabric of business operations, transcending traditional approaches and fostering a new level of efficiency, agility, and customer engagement.

In the future envisaged by this model, every enterprise, drawing inspiration from the success story of Enterprise GlobeTaste Bistro, is empowered to harness the transformative capabilities of AGI and ChatGPT. The integration of AI in business processes evolves from being a mere competitive edge to becoming an indispensable core component of business strategy and operations. This vision extends beyond the realm of aspiration into the domain of imminent realization, marking the commencement of an era where industries are not just modified but thoroughly revitalized through the power of AI.

In this new epoch, businesses are envisioned as dynamic, adaptive entities, thriving in a landscape where technological innovation is not just an enabler but a driving force. This era sees the emergence of enterprises that are not only participants in their respective industries but pioneers charting new territories in innovation, efficiency, and customer satisfaction. The legacy of Enterprise GlobeTaste Bistro thus becomes a beacon, illuminating the path toward a future where AI and human creativity coalesce to create unparalleled opportunities for growth and transformation.

In conclusion, the journey of Enterprise GlobeTaste Bistro is a narrative that encapsulates the transformative impact of AI across the spectrum of business and culinary arts. It is a story that resonates with the potential of AI to redefine the future of enterprises, signaling a new era of innovation and excellence where AI is the cornerstone of strategic development and creative expression.

World Bistro Enterprise
Comprehensive Operational Blueprint for GlobeTaste Bistro Restaurant

Strategic Framework for GlobeTaste Bistro Restaurant's Success

To effectively position and manage "GlobeTaste Bistro Restaurant" with a target revenue of around $1,792,800, we can draw upon a framework that includes analyzing similar successful restaurants, considering optimal locations, size, staffing, and other key operational aspects. Here's a guide to structure your approach:

Examples of Comparable Restaurants

Restaurant Type: GlobeTaste Bistro aligns with high-end dining establishments or popular mid-to-upscale casual dining restaurants. Examples include independent fine dining restaurants in major cities or successful regional casual dining chains.

Location: Urban areas in major cities with high foot traffic, business districts, or upscale neighborhoods. Tourist destinations or areas with high density of cultural or entertainment venues are ideal.

Key Operational Considerations

Size and Capacity: For fine dining, intimate settings with 50-100 seats; for casual upscale, larger spaces with 100-200 seats.

Menu and Pricing: Premium pricing for fine dining with unique, high-quality ingredients; diverse menu with a range of pricing for casual upscale.

Staff and Management: An experienced executive chef, skilled front-of-house team, and adequate staffing based on restaurant size.

Operational Efficiency

Efficient kitchen design, effective inventory management, and use of technology for reservations and customer management.

Specific examples for fine and casual upscale dining include location, size, staff numbers, and operational strategies.

Section 1: Enhancing GlobeTaste Bistro's Operational and Culinary Excellence

1. Customer Experience Enhancement: Investing in ambiance, updating the menu, and offering personalized services.
2. Leveraging Technology: Implementing advanced POS systems, using data analytics, and developing online platforms.
3. Community and Event Engagement: Hosting culinary events, participating in local festivals, and collaborating with local artists.
4. Strategic Marketing: Digital marketing strategies, customer reviews, and collaborations with influencers.
5. Cost Control and Financial Management: Managing supplier contracts, operational costs, and financial contingency plans.
6. Staff Training and Development: Regular training, positive work culture, and identifying talent for leadership roles.
7. Sustainability Practices: Implementing sustainable practices in sourcing and operations, and marketing these efforts.
8. Menu Diversification and Specialization: Offering special menus for dietary needs and experimenting with fusion cuisines.

9. Licensing and Permits: Staying updated with local regulations and exploring opportunities for additional permits.
10. Long-term Business Planning: Updating business plans regularly, considering expansion opportunities, and adapting to market changes.

Section 2: Maximizing Revenue and Customer Engagement

1. Diverse Revenue Streams: Introducing catering services, signature products, and gift cards.
2. Seasonal and Thematic Promotions: Creating seasonal menus and organizing themed dining experiences.
3. Strategic Alliances and Partnerships: Partnering with local businesses, food and beverage brands, and community initiatives.
4. Real Estate and Location Strategy: Evaluating relocation or opening a second location and the benefits of purchasing versus leasing.
5. Operational Excellence: Focusing on quality ingredients, streamlining kitchen operations, and consistent preparation.
6. Customer Feedback and Engagement: Collecting customer feedback and engaging on social media.
7. Staff Incentivization and Retention: Implementing staff incentive programs and offering career development opportunities.
8. Risk Management and Compliance: Ensuring comprehensive insurance coverage and compliance with regulations.
9. Financial Planning and Analysis: Conducting financial reviews, adjusting budgets, and forecasting for future growth.
10. Building a Strong Brand Identity: Developing a unique brand story, reinforcing the brand through marketing, and consistent customer service.

76

Section 3: Sustaining Long-term Growth and Adaptability

1. Enhancing Online Presence: SEO optimization, engaging content, and video marketing.
2. Culinary Innovations: Refreshing the menu with innovative dishes and hosting guest chefs.
3. Customer Loyalty and Retention: Creating loyalty programs and implementing a referral program.
4. Targeted Advertising and Promotions: Utilizing targeted advertising and special promotions to increase foot traffic.
5. Local Community Engagement: Participating in community events and sponsoring local activities.
6. Interior Design and Ambiance: Regularly updating interior decor, investing in comfortable furniture, and creating a unique dining atmosphere.
7. Staff Training and Professional Development: Providing opportunities for learning and growth within the company.
8. Health and Safety Standards: Maintaining high standards of cleanliness and hygiene.
9. Sustainability and Ethical Practices: Promoting sustainable and ethical sourcing practices.
10. Financial Management and Investment: Strategic investments in technology and managing cash flow effectively.

By integrating these comprehensive considerations into its operational strategy, "GlobeTaste Bistro Restaurant" can enhance its market position, customer satisfaction, and overall profitability, contributing significantly to achieving its revenue target.

Position and Manage the World Bistro Enterprise
The "Enterprise GlobeTaste Bistro" Restaurant

Main Section:

To effectively position and manage "GlobeTaste Bistro Restaurant" with a target revenue of around $1,792,800, we can draw upon a framework that includes analyzing similar successful restaurants, considering optimal locations, size, staffing, and other key operational aspects. Here's a guide to structure your approach:

Examples of Comparable Restaurants

Restaurant Type: Given the revenue target, GlobeTaste Bistro would likely align with either a high-end dining establishment or a popular mid-to-upscale casual dining restaurant. Examples could include independent fine dining restaurants in major cities or successful regional casual dining chains.

Location: Urban areas in major cities with high foot traffic, business districts, or upscale neighborhoods.

Tourist destinations or areas with a high density of cultural or entertainment venues.

Key Operational Considerations

Size and Capacity:

For fine dining: Smaller, more intimate settings with a focus on quality over quantity. Seating capacity could be around 50-100, depending on the space and layout.

For casual upscale: Larger spaces, potentially with 100-200 seats, including bar and outdoor seating areas.

Menu and Pricing:

Fine dining: Premium pricing with a focus on unique, high-quality ingredients, often with a specific cuisine focus or chef-driven concepts.

Casual upscale: A diverse menu with a range of pricing, aiming to cater to a wider audience without compromising on quality.

Staff and Management:

An experienced executive chef with a strong culinary background, preferably with recognition or awards.

A skilled and well-trained front-of-house team to ensure excellent customer service.

Adequate staffing based on restaurant size and expected customer flow.

78

Operational Efficiency:

Efficient kitchen design and workflow.
Effective inventory management to control costs.
Use of technology for reservations, order management, and customer relationship management.

Specific Examples

Fine Dining:

Location: Central business districts of cities like San Francisco, Los Angeles, or San Diego.
Size: Approximately 2,500 to 4,000 square feet.
Staff: Around 20-30 employees, including kitchen and front-of-house staff.

Casual Upscale Dining:

Location: Busy urban streets, shopping districts, or near entertainment venues.
Size: Approximately 4,000 to 6,000 square feet.
Staff: Around 30-50 employees, depending on the size and service model.

Additional Considerations

Market Research: Conduct detailed market research to understand the demographics, preferences, and spending habits of the target customer base.
Marketing and Branding: Develop a strong branding and marketing strategy to build a loyal customer base and attract new patrons.
Local Partnerships: Forge partnerships with local businesses, cultural institutions, or event venues to drive traffic.
Sustainability and Local Sourcing: Emphasize sustainability and locally sourced ingredients, which are increasingly important to consumers.

By aligning GlobeTaste Bistro with these operational benchmarks and learning from successful models in the industry, you can strategically position the restaurant to achieve the target revenue while maintaining a focus on quality, customer experience, and operational excellence.

Section 1:

Certainly, there are several additional considerations that can further optimize the success and revenue of "GlobeTaste Bistro Restaurant" with its target revenue of around $1,792,800:

Customer Experience Enhancement:

Invest in ambiance and decor to create a memorable dining atmosphere.
Regularly update the menu with innovative dishes to keep the dining experience fresh and exciting.
Offer personalized services, like custom meal options or special occasion arrangements.

Leveraging Technology:

Implement advanced POS systems for efficient order processing and inventory management.
Use data analytics to track customer preferences, peak hours, and popular menu items for better decision-making.
Develop a user-friendly website and mobile app for online reservations, orders, and promotions.

Community and Event Engagement:

Host culinary events, wine tasting sessions, or cooking classes to attract a diverse clientele.
Participate in local food festivals and community events for brand visibility.
Collaborate with local artists or musicians for regular entertainment nights.

Strategic Marketing:

Implement a robust digital marketing strategy including social media engagement and targeted online advertising.
Encourage customer reviews and referrals through loyalty programs and incentives.
Collaborate with food bloggers and influencers for wider exposure.

Cost Control and Financial Management:

Regularly review and optimize supplier contracts and purchasing strategies.
Monitor and manage operational costs such as utilities, staffing, and maintenance.
Develop a financial contingency plan to manage unforeseen expenses or downturns.

Staff Training and Development:

Invest in regular staff training to ensure high service standards.
Foster a positive work culture for better employee retention and productivity.
Identify and nurture talent within the team for leadership and specialized roles.

Sustainability Practices:

Implement eco-friendly practices in sourcing, waste management, and operations.
Market sustainability efforts to attract environmentally conscious customers.
Explore partnerships with sustainable suppliers and local farms.

Menu Diversification and Specialization:

Consider offering special menus for dietary needs like vegan, gluten-free, or allergy-friendly options.
Experiment with fusion cuisines or seasonal specialties to attract a broader customer base.

Licensing and Permits:

Stay updated with local regulations regarding health, safety, and business operations.
Explore opportunities for additional permits, like outdoor seating or extended hours.

Long-term Business Planning:

Regularly update the business plan to reflect market changes, business growth, and long-term goals.
Consider expansion opportunities, either through physical growth or by exploring new market segments.

By addressing these considerations, "GlobeTaste Bistro Restaurant" can not only aim to achieve its revenue target but also establish itself as a reputable and thriving entity in the competitive restaurant landscape.

Section 2:

Absolutely, here are additional considerations for "GlobeTaste Bistro Restaurant" to reach its revenue target and excel in the competitive restaurant industry:

Diverse Revenue Streams:

Introduce catering services for private events and corporate functions.
Develop a line of signature products for retail, such as sauces, baked goods, or branded merchandise.
Offer gift cards and premium membership programs.

Seasonal and Thematic Promotions:

Create seasonal menus to leverage fresh, local ingredients and attract repeat customers.
Organize themed dining experiences aligned with holidays, cultural events, or popular trends.

Strategic Alliances and Partnerships:

Partner with local businesses for cross-promotion, like hotels for guest dining options.
Collaborate with food and beverage brands for exclusive menu items or events.
Engage in community initiatives to build a strong local presence.

Real Estate and Location Strategy:

Consider the potential of relocating or opening a second location in a more lucrative area.
Evaluate the benefits of purchasing versus leasing restaurant space.

Operational Excellence:

Focus on high-quality ingredients and consistent preparation to ensure every dish meets high standards.
Streamline kitchen operations for speed and efficiency without compromising quality.

Customer Feedback and Engagement:

Regularly collect and analyze customer feedback for continuous improvement.
Engage with customers on social media and through email newsletters.

82

Staff Incentivization and Retention:

> Implement incentive programs for staff based on performance and customer feedback.
> Offer career development opportunities and competitive benefits to retain top talent.

Risk Management and Compliance:

> Ensure comprehensive insurance coverage for the restaurant.
> Stay compliant with all health, safety, and employment regulations.

Financial Planning and Analysis:

> Conduct regular financial reviews and adjust budgets to optimize profitability.
> Use forecasting models to plan for future growth or potential market changes.

Building a Strong Brand Identity:

> Develop a unique brand story and ethos that resonates with your target audience.
> Consistently reinforce the brand through marketing, menu design, staff training, and customer service.

By embracing these strategies, "GlobeTaste Bistro Restaurant" can not only aim for its revenue target but also build a sustainable, reputable, and beloved brand in the culinary world.

Section 3:

Certainly, there are additional nuanced considerations for "GlobeTaste Bistro Restaurant" that could further propel its success and help it reach its revenue target:

Enhancing Online Presence:

> Optimize the restaurant's website for search engines to increase visibility.
> Regularly update the website with engaging content like blogs, chef interviews, and behind-the-scenes stories.
> Leverage video marketing through platforms like YouTube to showcase the restaurant's ambiance, dishes, and special events.

Culinary Innovations:

Regularly refresh the menu with innovative dishes to keep the offerings exciting and new.
Experiment with global culinary trends and incorporate them into the menu.
Host guest chefs for limited-time special menus.

Customer Loyalty and Retention:

Create a loyalty program that rewards frequent diners with discounts, special offers, or exclusive experiences.

Implement a referral program to encourage existing customers to bring in new diners.

Targeted Advertising and Promotions:

Utilize targeted advertising on social media and Google to reach potential customers in your geographic area.
Collaborate with local influencers or food critics to increase exposure.
Offer special promotions during slow hours or days to increase foot traffic.

Local Community Engagement:

Participate in local community events to increase brand awareness.
Sponsor local sports teams or events.
Collaborate with local schools or charities for community-focused events.

Interior Design and Ambiance:

Regularly update the interior decor to keep the ambiance fresh and inviting.
Invest in comfortable and stylish furniture to enhance the dining experience.
Use lighting, music, and art to create a unique and pleasant dining atmosphere.

Staff Training and Professional Development:

Conduct regular training sessions for staff to improve service quality.
Provide opportunities for staff to learn and grow within the company.
Foster a positive and inclusive work culture.

Health and Safety Standards:

Maintain high standards of cleanliness and hygiene.
Stay up-to-date with health and safety regulations to ensure compliance.

Sustainability and Ethical Practices:

Implement sustainable practices in sourcing, energy use, and waste management.
Promote ethical practices such as fair trade and animal welfare in sourcing ingredients.

Financial Management and Investment:

Consider strategic investments in technology, equipment, or renovations to improve efficiency and customer experience.
Manage cash flow effectively and plan for long-term financial stability.

By integrating these considerations into its operational strategy, "GlobeTaste Bistro Restaurant" can enhance its market position, customer satisfaction, and overall profitability, contributing significantly to achieving its revenue target.

World Bistro Enterprise

Vision Paper

The Future of Enterprises Revolutionized by AGI and ChatGPT – The "Enterprise GlobeTaste Bistro" Paradigm

World Bistro Enterprise
Vision Paper
The Future of Enterprises Revolutionized by AGI and ChatGPT –
The "Enterprise GlobeTaste Bistro" Paradigm

Vision Paper: The Future of Enterprises Revolutionized by AGI and ChatGPT – The "Enterprise GlobeTaste Bistro" Paradigm

Introduction: A Culinary Renaissance in the Digital Age

In an era where technological advancements are not just altering but revolutionizing landscapes, the culinary world finds itself at the epicenter of a profound metamorphosis. This transformation, driven by the relentless pace of innovation, has ushered in a new age of culinary renaissance. "Enterprise GlobeTaste Bistro" emerges as the vanguard of this revolution, exemplifying an unparalleled synthesis of gastronomic brilliance and technological ingenuity. This vision paper embarks on an exploratory journey into the transformative world of Enterprise GlobeTaste Bistro, a beacon that not only redefines the culinary experience through the lens of technology but also stands as a paradigmatic example for industries worldwide. Here, we delve into a narrative that transcends traditional culinary confines, illustrating how the fusion of AI and culinary arts heralds a new era for businesses across various sectors. This odyssey unveils a future where technology is seamlessly integrated with culinary creativity, reimagining the realm of gastronomy and setting a precedent for how businesses can leverage AI to innovate, evolve, and excel.

I. The Genesis of Culinary Innovation

Enterprise GlobeTaste Bistro's inception was not just a leap into the culinary domain but a paradigm shift in the use of technology for culinary excellence. Starting as a concept that intertwined the prowess of Gourmet Genius, a digital culinary assistant, with the AGI-ChatGPT Tax Platform, it broke new ground. This combination of culinary finesse with advanced AI analytics laid the foundation for a versatile and comprehensive business model. This model spans the spectrum of culinary services, including high-end restaurant experiences, bespoke catering services, innovative home-based food delivery, adaptable small to medium-scale delivery services, and expansive corporate-business food delivery systems.

This innovative approach extended beyond the mere preparation of exquisite dishes. It delved into the realms of market analysis, customer behavior, and competitive strategy, utilizing advanced AI algorithms to decipher and navigate the complex culinary business landscape. By integrating these elements, Enterprise GlobeTaste Bistro set a new standard in the culinary industry, blending the art of cooking with the science of technology.

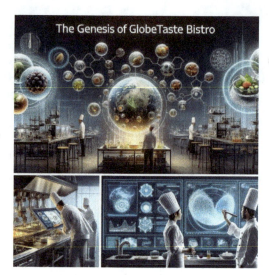

II. The Evolution of Gourmet Genius

Originally conceptualized as a digital tool for quick, budget-friendly recipe curation, Gourmet Genius evolved into a sophisticated culinary architect under the umbrella of Enterprise GlobeTaste Bistro. This evolution was marked by its ability to not only generate recipes but also to adapt to and address the multifaceted demands of a diverse culinary market.

As Gourmet Genius expanded its capabilities, it became an indispensable tool for strategic business planning and culinary innovation. Its growth from a recipe assistant to a comprehensive culinary consultant was instrumental in shaping the business strategy of Enterprise GlobeTaste Bistro. This transformation was characterized by its ability to analyze market trends, forecast consumer preferences, and generate innovative culinary concepts, thereby becoming a cornerstone in the development of a dynamic and responsive culinary enterprise.

Gourmet Genius' growth mirrored the changing landscape of the culinary world, where the demand for personalized, innovative, and accessible culinary experiences was on the rise. Its role in the conceptualization of Enterprise GlobeTaste Bistro exemplified how technology could be leveraged to not only enhance the culinary experience but also to revolutionize the way culinary businesses operate.

III. The Emergence of Enterprise GlobeTaste Bistro

The inception of Enterprise GlobeTaste Bistro heralded a new era in the culinary narrative, symbolizing more than the birth of a culinary conglomerate; it represented the fusion of technological prowess with gastronomic artistry. Within this enterprise, each business component - the flagship restaurant, the versatile catering service, the innovative home-based food delivery, the adaptive small to medium-scale delivery, and the expansive corporate-business delivery - was not merely a separate entity but a cog in a larger, intricately connected mechanism.

The design and implementation of each component were underpinned by meticulous consideration of market dynamics, consumer behavior, and strategic financial planning. The utilization of AGI-ChatGPT Tax Platform was pivotal, revolutionizing not just business strategy but also the execution of location intelligence. This platform provided deep insights into market trends, consumer preferences, and tax implications, enabling the Bistro to optimize its operations and tailor its services to different market segments effectively.

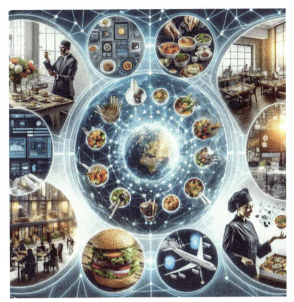

Moreover, the Bistro embraced the concept of a 'living enterprise' – one that adapts, learns, and evolves in real-time, responding agilely to the ever-changing culinary landscape. This adaptability was powered by AGI's capability to process vast amounts of data, identify patterns, and predict market shifts, ensuring that the Bistro remained at the forefront of culinary innovation and customer satisfaction.

IV. The Culinary Revolution: A Future Envisioned

The future envisioned by the emergence of Enterprise GlobeTaste Bistro is one where culinary creations and business operations are seamlessly interwoven with technological innovation. This future is not confined to the realms of imaginative speculation but is a tangible reality within grasp. In this future, culinary masterpieces are not just crafted in state-of-the-art kitchens but are the products of a harmonious blend of AI-driven analytics, creative gastronomy, and strategic business acumen.

In this revolutionary era, Enterprise GlobeTaste Bistro stands as a testament to the power of technology in transforming the culinary experience. The platform's ability to perform real-time, comprehensive tax analysis, and strategic location selection exemplifies how technology can streamline and enhance business operations. The potential extends beyond operational efficiency; it signifies a paradigm shift in how culinary businesses engage with their customers, understand their preferences, and deliver unparalleled gastronomic experiences.

Furthermore, this vision of the future posits Enterprise GlobeTaste Bistro as a hub of culinary innovation, where AI not only assists in crafting recipes but also in conceptualizing new dining concepts, exploring uncharted gastronomic territories, and creating unique, personalized customer experiences. The Bistro becomes a symbol of what is possible when technology and human creativity converge - a place where each meal is a fusion of global flavors, crafted with precision and personalized to individual tastes.

V. The Culinary Canvas: An AI-Powered Masterpiece

In the envisioned future, Enterprise GlobeTaste Bistro transcends the traditional culinary canvas, elevating it to a global stage powered by the advanced capabilities of AI. This new canvas is not just a platform for showcasing culinary skills but a confluence of technology, art, and customer engagement. The Bistro's diverse business models represent a microcosm of this expansive canvas, each element reflecting the power of AI to transform culinary experiences.

The comprehensive tax analysis and strategic location selection, done in seconds, are just the beginning. The platform's capabilities extend to predictive customer preference analysis, supply chain optimization, and even real-time menu customization based on dynamic market trends. Here, technology does not overshadow the culinary art; instead, it enhances it, allowing chefs to focus on creativity and innovation while AI handles the intricacies of business operations.

This AI-powered culinary canvas paves the way for a new era in dining experiences. It enables the creation of dishes that are not only gastronomically exquisite but also tailored to the nuanced preferences of a diverse clientele. The Bistro becomes a place where technology and tradition blend harmoniously, where every dish tells a story of global flavors, crafted with precision and a deep understanding of culinary artistry.

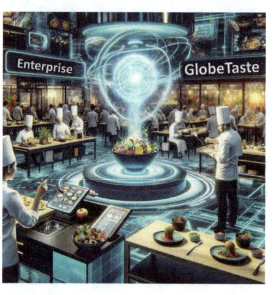

VI. A Revolution Beyond the Kitchen: Comprehensive Business Transformation

The transformative journey of Enterprise GlobeTaste Bistro is not confined to the realms of the kitchen; its implications ripple across the entire spectrum of business operations. The Bistro's model, powered by AGI and ChatGPT, illuminates the potential for AI to revolutionize aspects of business that extend far beyond culinary creativity. This model serves as a blueprint for an overarching business transformation, impacting areas such as tax filing, location analytics, and comprehensive business strategy.

The platform's capabilities in conducting real-time scenario analysis revolutionize decision-making processes for businesses. This feature, exemplified in the Bistro's operation, demonstrates how companies can navigate complex scenarios with ease and precision, making informed decisions that traditionally required extensive time and expertise.

Furthermore, the integration of intuitive AI-driven decision-making tools enables businesses of all scales to operate with a level of efficiency and strategic insight that was previously unattainable. Small businesses, in particular, can leverage these tools to compete on a larger scale, accessing analytics and insights that empower them to make decisions on par with their larger counterparts.

In addition, the Bistro's innovative approach to tax filing and location analytics offers a paradigm shift in financial and operational strategy. By utilizing AI to decipher complex tax laws and analyze the implications of various locations, businesses can optimize their operations, ensuring compliance and efficiency in a way that is both cost-effective and time-saving.

This revolution extends to customer engagement and market positioning strategies. Enterprise GlobeTaste Bistro's model demonstrates how AI can be used to understand and predict customer behavior, enabling businesses to tailor their services and products to meet evolving market demands. This level of customer insight and personalization fosters deeper connections between businesses and their clientele, driving growth and loyalty.

Conclusion: A New Epoch in Culinary and Business Innovation

The odyssey of Enterprise GlobeTaste Bistro from a nascent concept to a trailblazing enterprise heralds the beginning of a new epoch in both culinary and business history. This evolution represents more than a culinary success; it symbolizes the dawn of a transformative era where AI's potential and culinary creativity converge to redefine industry norms. As we stand at the precipice of this era, we are witnessing the reshaping of the culinary world and beyond, driven by the synergistic fusion of technology and human ingenuity.

This transformation transcends the confines of the culinary industry. The model established by Enterprise GlobeTaste Bistro serves as a pioneering blueprint for businesses across a multitude of sectors, showcasing the vast

potential that unfolds when technological innovation aligns with human creativity and strategic insight. It is a model that demonstrates how AI can be seamlessly woven into the fabric of business operations, transcending traditional approaches and fostering a new level of efficiency, agility, and customer engagement.

In the future envisaged by this model, every enterprise, drawing inspiration from the success story of Enterprise GlobeTaste Bistro, is empowered to harness the transformative capabilities of AGI and ChatGPT. The integration of AI in business processes evolves from being a mere competitive edge to becoming an indispensable core component of business strategy and operations. This vision extends beyond the realm of aspiration into the domain of imminent realization, marking the commencement of an era where industries are not just modified but thoroughly revitalized through the power of AI.

In this new epoch, businesses are envisioned as dynamic, adaptive entities, thriving in a landscape where technological innovation is not just an enabler but a driving force. This era sees the emergence of enterprises that are not only participants in their respective industries but pioneers charting new territories in innovation, efficiency, and customer satisfaction. The legacy of Enterprise GlobeTaste Bistro thus becomes a beacon, illuminating the path toward a future where AI and human creativity coalesce to create unparalleled opportunities for growth and transformation.

In conclusion, the journey of Enterprise GlobeTaste Bistro is a narrative that encapsulates the transformative impact of AI across the spectrum of business and culinary arts. It is a story that resonates with the potential of AI to redefine the future of enterprises, signaling a new era of innovation and excellence where AI is the cornerstone of strategic development and creative expression.

World Bistro Enterprise
Vision Paper
Transformative Impact of AGI and ChatGPT Across Industries
The "Enterprise GlobeTaste Bistro" Paradigm

Vision Paper: Transformative Impact of AGI and ChatGPT Across Industries

I. Introduction: The Dawn of a New Enterprise Era

In an epoch where the fusion of technology with everyday life is more pronounced than ever, the emergence of Artificial General Intelligence (AGI) and ChatGPT stands as a watershed moment in the history of industry and commerce. These technological marvels have not only catalyzed a profound revolution within the culinary realm, as exemplified by the pioneering Enterprise GlobeTaste Bistro, but their influence extends far beyond, permeating various sectors across the global business landscape. This vision paper embarks on a comprehensive exploration of how the integration of AGI and ChatGPT is fundamentally redefining the operational, strategic, and experiential aspects of industries worldwide.

We stand at the threshold of a new enterprise era, one characterized by the symbiotic integration of artificial intelligence with human creativity and insight. In this era, AGI and ChatGPT are not merely tools or adjuncts to existing business practices; they are transformative agents that are reshaping the core of how industries operate, innovate, and interact with their stakeholders. This narrative extension delves into the multifaceted implications of these technologies across diverse sectors, illuminating how they are heralding a new age of innovation, efficiency, and strategic prowess.

From healthcare, education, and finance to manufacturing, retail, and environmental sustainability, the ripple effects of AGI and ChatGPT's integration are vast and profound. These technologies are enabling businesses to transcend traditional limitations, offering new vistas of opportunity and growth. They are reshaping the way enterprises think about customer engagement, operational efficiency, and strategic planning, instilling a culture of data-driven decision-making and personalized service delivery.

This paper aims to unfold the tapestry of this new enterprise era, drawing insights from the success of Enterprise GlobeTaste Bistro and extending these learnings to paint a picture of a future where AI is deeply embedded in the fabric of business operations. It is a future where the boundaries between artificial intelligence and human enterprise are blurred, giving rise to a harmonious blend of technology-driven efficiency and human-centric innovation.

As we navigate through the pages of this vision paper, we invite readers to envision a world where AGI and ChatGPT are not just technological phenomena but essential components of the modern business ethos. A world where the transformative impact of these technologies is ubiquitously evident across industries, marking the beginning of an era where every enterprise is empowered to reach new heights of success and innovation.

II. Beyond Culinary Boundaries: A Universal Transformation

The remarkable success and innovation of Enterprise GlobeTaste Bistro transcend the confines of culinary arts, providing a versatile blueprint for a myriad of industries. The integration of AGI and ChatGPT within the Bistro's operations epitomizes a groundbreaking model of efficiency, innovation, and strategic foresight, offering valuable insights and strategies that can be replicated and adapted across diverse sectors.

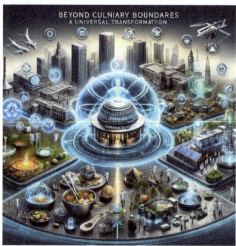

Expanding the Culinary Model to Other Industries:

Cross-Industry Efficiency: The operational efficiencies achieved at Enterprise GlobeTaste Bistro through AI, such as optimized workflow and resource management, can inspire similar advancements in sectors like healthcare, manufacturing, and logistics. These industries can adopt AI-driven approaches to streamline their processes, enhance productivity, and reduce operational costs.

Innovative Customer Engagement: The way in which Enterprise GlobeTaste Bistro employs ChatGPT to engage and understand its clientele, customizing dining experiences based on preferences and feedback, sets a precedent for customer relationship management. Retail, service industries, and even sectors like banking can leverage this model to deepen customer engagement and personalize their services.

Strategic Decision-Making and Planning: The strategic use of AGI at the Bistro for menu planning, market analysis, and business expansion serves as a model for other industries to incorporate AI into their strategic planning. This approach can significantly benefit sectors like real estate, finance, and environmental management, where strategic foresight and data-driven decision-making are crucial.

Enterprise GlobeTaste Bistro as a Universal Blueprint:

The methodologies and technologies harnessed by Enterprise GlobeTaste Bistro provide a comprehensive framework that can be applied universally. Businesses in various sectors can draw inspiration from the Bistro's use of AGI and ChatGPT to not only enhance their operational capabilities but also to innovate and redefine their industry standards.

Adapting AI for Industry-Specific Challenges: Industries can customize AI applications to address their unique challenges and opportunities, much like how the Bistro tailored AI solutions to enhance culinary experiences and operational efficiency.

Harnessing Data for Competitive Advantage: The model of utilizing data analytics for business growth and customer satisfaction at Enterprise GlobeTaste Bistro can be replicated across sectors. By harnessing data effectively, businesses can gain a competitive edge, uncover new opportunities, and make more informed decisions.

Cultivating a Culture of Innovation: Enterprise GlobeTaste Bistro's success story exemplifies the importance of fostering a culture of innovation. Businesses can embrace this ethos, encouraging experimentation and leveraging AI to push the boundaries of what's possible in their respective fields.

By extending the innovative model of Enterprise GlobeTaste Bistro across various industries, businesses can revolutionize their operations, customer relations, and strategic planning. The Bistro's journey exemplifies how the integration of AI can transform not just a single enterprise but can set a new trajectory for industries at large.

III. The Healthcare Revolution: Informed by Culinary Precision and Innovation

The intersection of AGI and ChatGPT technologies with healthcare, inspired by the advancements at Enterprise GlobeTaste Bistro, heralds a new era of precision, efficiency, and personalized care. The integration of these technologies in healthcare mirrors the innovative approaches employed in the culinary world, promising a transformative impact on patient care, medical research, and healthcare administration.

General Impact of AGI and ChatGPT in Healthcare:

Precision Diagnostics: AGI, with its capacity for deep learning and data analysis, can revolutionize diagnostics, offering precise and rapid patient assessments. This mirrors the meticulous ingredient analysis and flavor profiling at Enterprise GlobeTaste Bistro, where AI aids in creating perfect culinary compositions.

Personalized Care: Just as ChatGPT at the Bistro enables tailored customer interactions, in healthcare, it can provide personalized health advice and patient communication, enhancing the patient experience and ensuring better health outcomes.

Accelerated Medical Research: AGI's ability to process vast datasets can expedite drug discovery and medical research, similar to how Enterprise GlobeTaste Bistro utilizes AI for recipe development and culinary trend analysis.

Relation to Enterprise GlobeTaste Bistro's Technologies:

Data-Driven Decision Making: The Bistro's model of using AGI for analyzing customer preferences and culinary trends can be adapted to healthcare for understanding patient data and medical histories, leading to more informed treatment decisions.

Operational Efficiency: The operational efficiency seen in Enterprise GlobeTaste Bistro, achieved through AI-powered logistics and management, can inspire similar efficiency in hospital administration and resource allocation.

Scenario Analysis and Planning: The Bistro's use of ChatGPT for what-if scenarios and strategic planning can be paralleled in healthcare for emergency response planning, health crisis management, and predictive healthcare analytics.

By adopting the innovative approaches of Enterprise GlobeTaste Bistro, healthcare institutions can achieve a higher level of patient care and operational efficiency. The fusion of culinary precision and AI-driven innovation in the Bistro serves as a blueprint for a healthcare revolution, where technology and human expertise combine to create a more responsive, efficient, and patient-centric healthcare system.

IV. Retail and E-Commerce: Personalized Shopping Experiences Inspired by Culinary Innovation

Drawing inspiration from Enterprise GlobeTaste Bistro's use of AGI and ChatGPT, the retail and e-commerce sector stands on the cusp of a significant transformation. The integration of these advanced technologies promises to redefine the shopping experience, mirroring the personalization and efficiency that characterizes the Bistro's service.

General Impact of AGI and ChatGPT in Retail and E-Commerce:

Enhanced Customer Service: AGI can analyze customer preferences and shopping habits, similar to how it identifies dining preferences at the Bistro. This data can be used to provide personalized shopping recommendations and customer support.

Inventory Management and Supply Chain Optimization: ChatGPT's capabilities in managing complex data can be applied to streamline inventory control, much like the efficient supply chain management at the Bistro. This can lead to more efficient stocking strategies and reduced waste.

Dynamic Pricing and Marketing: AGI can assist in dynamic pricing strategies by analyzing market trends and consumer behavior, a technique akin to the Bistro's approach in menu pricing and promotional offers.

Relation to Enterprise GlobeTaste Bistro's Technologies:

Customized Product Recommendations: The Bistro's model of using AGI to tailor culinary experiences can inspire e-commerce platforms to offer personalized product suggestions, enhancing the shopping experience for each customer.

AI-driven Insights for Business Strategy: Just as Enterprise GlobeTaste Bistro leverages AI for strategic decisions and menu optimization, retail businesses can use similar insights to develop strategic business decisions, from marketing campaigns to store layouts.

Interactive and Responsive Platforms: ChatGPT's role in engaging customers at the Bistro can be mirrored in online retail, where AI-powered chatbots provide real-time assistance, replicating the attentive service of a gourmet restaurant.

By embracing the technological advancements exemplified by Enterprise GlobeTaste Bistro, the retail and e-commerce sector can enhance customer engagement, streamline operations, and create more responsive and personalized shopping experiences. This approach, where technology is harmoniously blended with customer service, sets a new standard in retail, much like the Bistro's transformative impact in the culinary world.

V. Financial Services: AI-Powered Financial Planning Modeled on Culinary Expertise

The revolution in financial services, inspired by the innovations at Enterprise GlobeTaste Bistro, showcases how AGI and ChatGPT can profoundly transform the industry. The Bistro's model of utilizing advanced AI for strategic decision-making and operational efficiency presents a blueprint for the financial sector to enhance its services.

General Impact of AGI and ChatGPT in Financial Services:

Advanced Investment Strategies: AGI, with its deep learning capabilities, can analyze market data and consumer trends to devise sophisticated investment strategies. This mirrors the Bistro's use of AI to understand culinary trends and customer preferences for menu development.

Personalized Financial Advice: ChatGPT's ability to interact and provide tailored responses can be adapted to offer personalized financial planning and advice, much like the customized culinary recommendations at the Bistro.

Risk Assessment and Compliance: AGI's predictive analytics can be vital in assessing financial risks and ensuring compliance, akin to how the Bistro utilizes AI for regulatory adherence and risk management in its operations.

Relation to Enterprise GlobeTaste Bistro's Technologies:

Real-Time Market Analysis: The real-time analytics used at Enterprise GlobeTaste Bistro for market and customer analysis can be paralleled in financial services for up-to-the-minute market trends and investment opportunities.

Operational Efficiency in Financial Management: The operational efficiencies achieved by the Bistro through AI, from inventory management to cost analysis, can inspire financial institutions to streamline their processes, from transaction processing to customer service.

Scenario Planning and Forecasting: The Bistro's use of ChatGPT for scenario analysis and strategic planning can be translated into financial forecasting and scenario planning in banking and investment, offering foresight and preparedness in an ever-changing financial landscape.

By adopting the AI-driven strategies exemplified by Enterprise GlobeTaste Bistro, financial services can achieve a higher level of precision, personalization, and efficiency. The integration of these technologies into the financial sector means more informed investment decisions, tailored financial advice, and robust risk management, transforming the way financial institutions operate and interact with their clients.

VI. Education and Training: A Recipe for Personalized Learning

The transformative application of AGI and ChatGPT in the field of education, drawing inspiration from the technological ingenuity at Enterprise GlobeTaste Bistro, presents a future where learning is deeply personalized, dynamic, and responsive to the needs of each individual student.

General Impact of AGI and ChatGPT in Education:

Personalized Learning Experiences: Just as AGI tailors culinary experiences at Enterprise GlobeTaste Bistro, it can be utilized to customize education pathways, adapting to the unique learning styles, speeds, and interests of students.

Dynamic Curriculum Development: ChatGPT's ability to analyze and interpret vast amounts of data can support educators in developing curricula that are more aligned with current trends, student needs, and global perspectives.

Interactive and Engaging Learning: AGI can create interactive and engaging learning environments, reminiscent of the immersive culinary experiences offered at the Bistro, thereby enhancing student engagement and learning outcomes.

Relation to Enterprise GlobeTaste Bistro's Technologies:

Tailored Educational Content: The Bistro's use of AGI to customize menus and culinary experiences can inspire the development of educational content that is tailored to individual learning objectives, much like a chef curates a menu to suit diverse palates.

AI-driven Analytics for Performance Improvement: Just as Enterprise GlobeTaste Bistro employs AI to analyze customer feedback and improve its offerings, educational institutions can use similar analytics to evaluate student performance and adapt teaching methods accordingly.

Interactive Learning Scenarios: ChatGPT, used at the Bistro for customer interaction and engagement, can be adapted in educational settings to create interactive scenarios, simulations, and problem-solving exercises, making learning more immersive and effective.

By integrating the innovative approaches used at Enterprise GlobeTaste Bistro into education, learning can be transformed into a more personalized, engaging, and effective process. The Bistro's model of using AI to enhance customer experience serves as a blueprint for how educational institutions can employ these technologies to revolutionize teaching and learning, making education more adaptable, responsive, and aligned with the needs of the digital age.

VII. Manufacturing and Production: Efficiency Reimagined Inspired by Culinary Excellence

The transformative influence of Enterprise GlobeTaste Bistro extends into the manufacturing and production sector, offering a blueprint for how AGI and ChatGPT can revolutionize these industries. Drawing parallels with the Bistro's utilization of AI for operational efficiency and innovation, the manufacturing sector can experience a significant shift in its production processes and overall business model.

General Impact of AGI and ChatGPT in Manufacturing and Production:

Enhanced Production Efficiency: AGI can optimize production lines and processes, similar to how it streamlines kitchen operations at the Bistro, leading to increased productivity and reduced waste.

Predictive Maintenance and Quality Control: The predictive analytics capability of AGI, akin to the Bistro's anticipatory customer service models, can be used for proactive maintenance scheduling and quality assurance in manufacturing.

Supply Chain Optimization: ChatGPT's ability to manage complex data sets can improve supply chain logistics, drawing on the Bistro's efficient ingredient sourcing and inventory management.

Relation to Enterprise GlobeTaste Bistro's Technologies:

Data-Driven Process Optimization: The AI-driven approach used at Enterprise GlobeTaste Bistro for optimizing culinary processes and menu offerings can inspire manufacturers to leverage similar data analytics for process refinement and product development.

AI-Assisted Operational Decision-Making: The Bistro's use of AGI for making strategic operational decisions, from menu changes to staffing, can be adapted in manufacturing for decisions related to production planning, resource allocation, and market responsiveness.

Customization and Personalization: Just as the Bistro personalizes dining experiences, manufacturers can use AGI and ChatGPT to offer greater product customization, aligning production closely with consumer preferences and market demands.

By integrating the advanced AI applications exemplified by Enterprise GlobeTaste Bistro, the manufacturing and production industry can achieve unprecedented levels of efficiency, precision, and adaptability. This integration signifies a move towards smarter, more responsive manufacturing practices, where AI-driven insights drive innovation and operational excellence.

VIII. Environmental Sustainability: AI-Driven Conservation Strategies Informed by Culinary Innovation

The paradigm established by Enterprise GlobeTaste Bistro in utilizing AGI and ChatGPT extends into the realm of environmental sustainability. The Bistro's approach to resource optimization and strategic location analysis offers valuable insights for environmental conservation efforts, demonstrating how AI can be a powerful tool in developing sustainable practices.

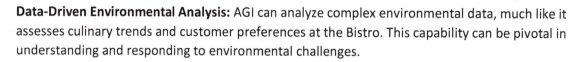

General Impact of AGI and ChatGPT in Environmental Sustainability:

Data-Driven Environmental Analysis: AGI can analyze complex environmental data, much like it assesses culinary trends and customer preferences at the Bistro. This capability can be pivotal in understanding and responding to environmental challenges.

Sustainable Resource Management: Drawing from the Bistro's efficient use of ingredients and minimization of waste, AGI can aid in optimizing resource utilization in various industries, promoting more sustainable practices.

Climate Change Mitigation Strategies: ChatGPT's ability to process and interpret vast datasets can support the development of effective climate change mitigation strategies, informed by predictive analytics.

Relation to Enterprise GlobeTaste Bistro's Technologies:

Efficient Operational Models for Sustainability: The operational efficiency achieved by the Bistro, facilitated by AI in inventory and supply chain management, provides a model for other industries to minimize their environmental footprint.

AI-Assisted Sustainability Planning: The strategic decision-making process at Enterprise GlobeTaste Bistro, guided by AGI, can inspire similar approaches in environmental planning, where AI helps in crafting long-term sustainability strategies and policies.

Scenario Analysis for Environmental Impact: The Bistro's use of ChatGPT for scenario analysis can be adapted to evaluate the environmental impact of various actions, aiding in the development of more sustainable business practices and environmental policies.

By integrating the AI-driven strategies exemplified at Enterprise GlobeTaste Bistro, industries focused on environmental sustainability can achieve greater efficiency and effectiveness in their efforts. This approach not only promotes a more sustainable business model but also contributes to broader environmental conservation goals, showcasing the potential of AI as a tool for positive environmental change.

IX. Conclusion: A Future Shaped by AI

As we project our gaze into the future, one where Artificial General Intelligence (AGI) and ChatGPT become foundational elements across various industries, we envisage a world undergoing profound transformation. This transformation is characterized by enhanced efficiency, deep personalization, and strategic foresight, reshaping the very essence of how businesses operate and interact with their environment. The pioneering example set by Enterprise GlobeTaste Bistro is just the inception of a much grander narrative, one where technology extends beyond its conventional roles to become an indispensable pillar in the evolution of global enterprises.

In this imminent future, businesses transcend their traditional definitions to become dynamic ecosystems. They are no longer static entities but adaptive, evolving organisms that grow and innovate through the integration of AI. This new era, illuminated by the success of Enterprise GlobeTaste Bistro, showcases a world where AI is not merely an add-on but a core component driving business strategies and operations. It's a future where the boundaries between artificial intelligence and human ingenuity blur, giving rise to a symbiotic relationship that fosters unprecedented levels of innovation and efficiency.

In this vision, every enterprise, regardless of size or sector, emerges as a testament to innovation, each strategy shaped by AI-driven insights. This paradigm shift signifies a move towards a smarter, more responsive business landscape, where AI empowers organizations to not only anticipate but also shape market trends and consumer needs. The integration of AGI and ChatGPT catalyzes a revolution in industry milestones, steering them towards a future that is not only more efficient and productive but also more sustainable and conscientious.

This is not a speculative or distant dream; it's a rapidly materializing reality, marking the dawn of an era where industries are not just reimagined but entirely revitalized through the transformative power of AI. As we welcome this new era, we embrace a world where innovation is continuous, insights are AI-driven, and every business decision is a step towards a smarter, more interconnected, and sustainable future. The journey of Enterprise GlobeTaste Bistro, therefore, stands as a beacon, signaling the limitless possibilities and the bright future that awaits the world of business and industry, powered by the revolutionary capabilities of AGI and ChatGPT.

World Bistro Enterprise
Vision Paper
AI-Driven Innovations in Societal Engagement
Title: "AI Empowerment in Civic and Community Frontiers"
The "Enterprise GlobeTaste Bistro" Paradigm

Vision Paper Series: AI-Driven Innovations in Societal Engagement
Title: "AI Empowerment in Civic and Community Frontiers"
By: Dr. Masoud Nikravesh

Introduction to the Series

In an era marked by rapid technological advancement, the advent of Artificial General Intelligence (AGI) and ChatGPT is not just transforming business and industry but is also reshaping the landscape of civic engagement and community support. This series of vision papers delves into three distinct but interconnected domains where AI is poised to make significant contributions: Political Contribution Investment Advising, Ballot Assistance, and Community Aid Services, particularly in immigration in the USA. Drawing inspiration from the success of Enterprise GlobeTaste Bistro in integrating AI for customer-centric solutions, these papers explore the transformative potential of AGI and ChatGPT in enhancing democratic participation, voter empowerment, and community support.

I. Political Contribution Investment Advisor: Navigating the Political Terrain with AI

Exploring the integration of AI in the realm of political finance, this paper discusses how AGI and ChatGPT can redefine political contributions, offering strategic, data-driven insights for donors, akin to the culinary innovations at Enterprise GlobeTaste Bistro.

II. Ballot Helper: Democratizing Voting in the Digital Age

Focusing on the American political system, this vision paper examines how AGI and ChatGPT can revolutionize the voting process, providing citizens with enhanced tools for understanding ballots, issues, and candidates, drawing parallels with the customer-centric approach of Enterprise GlobeTaste Bistro.

III. Mutual Aid Services and Immigration Aid: AI-Driven Community Assistance

This paper explores the potential of AGI and ChatGPT in revolutionizing mutual aid services, particularly in the context of immigration aid in the USA. It highlights how AI can offer unparalleled support and guidance to those navigating complex legal and societal landscapes, reflecting the innovations seen at Enterprise GlobeTaste Bistro.

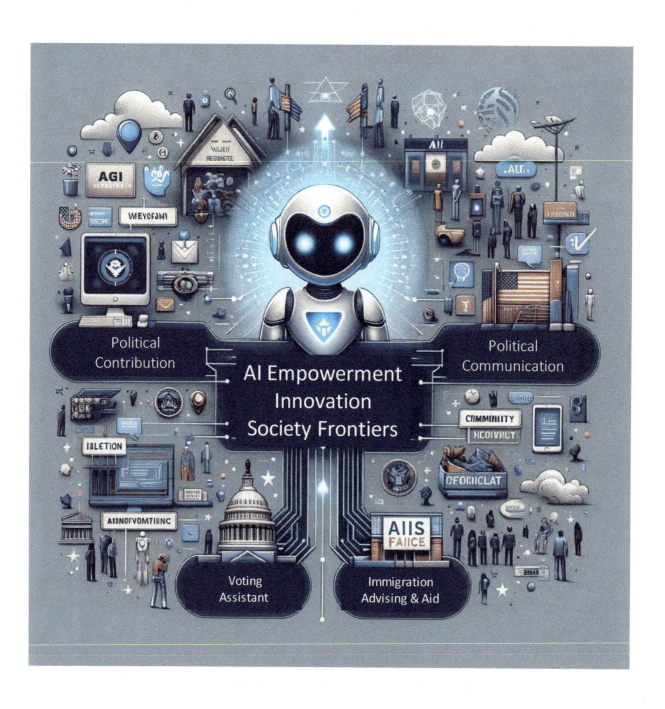

Section 1: Vision Paper: Transformative Impact of AGI and ChatGPT in Political Engagement
Case (1): Political Contribution Investment Advisor –
Revolutionizing Political Finance with AI
The "Enterprise GlobeTaste Bistro" Paradigm

Section 1: Vision Paper: Transformative Impact of AGI and ChatGPT in Political Engagement
Case (1): Political Contribution Investment Advisor – Revolutionizing Political Finance with AI

Introduction: A New Frontier in Political Engagement

As the political landscape evolves, the integration of Artificial General Intelligence (AGI) and ChatGPT heralds a significant transformation in political finance. This vision paper delves into the potential of these technologies to revolutionize the way individuals and organizations approach political contributions, offering a strategic and data-driven methodology akin to the innovations seen in Enterprise GlobeTaste Bistro.

I. General Impact of AGI and ChatGPT in Political Finance:

- **Strategic Contribution Analysis**: AGI can analyze historical political trends, campaign effectiveness, and policy impacts, guiding donors to make contributions that align with their political and social objectives.

- **Personalized Donor Advice:** Leveraging ChatGPT's conversational AI, individuals can receive personalized guidance on political contributions, considering their values, the political climate, and the potential impact of their contributions.

II. Relation to Enterprise GlobeTaste Bistro's Technologies:

- **Data-Driven Decision Making:** Similar to how Enterprise GlobeTaste Bistro employs AGI to tailor dining experiences and menu selections, AGI in political finance can provide strategic insights for donors, optimizing their contributions based on predictive analytics and trend analysis.

- **Customized Engagement Strategies:** Drawing parallels with ChatGPT's role at the Bistro in enhancing customer engagement, this technology can be utilized to communicate with potential donors, offering tailored suggestions and insights into political campaigns and issues.

III. Enhancing Transparency and Accountability:

- **Transparent Contribution Tracking:** AGI can be employed to ensure transparency in political contributions, akin to the Bistro's use of technology in transparently managing customer data and preferences.

- **Ethical Compliance Monitoring:** Utilizing AI to monitor and report political contributions can aid in adhering to legal and ethical standards, mirroring the Bistro's commitment to regulatory compliance and ethical business practices.

IV. Impact on Political Advocacy and Campaign Effectiveness:

- **Empowering Political Campaigns:** Just as AGI and ChatGPT enhance operational efficiency at Enterprise GlobeTaste Bistro, they can assist political campaigns in strategizing outreach, optimizing resource allocation, and enhancing voter engagement strategies.

- **Informed Voter Engagement:** Utilizing AI to educate and inform voters about political issues, candidates, and the impact of policies, paralleling the Bistro's approach in educating customers about culinary choices and practices.

V. Conclusion: AI as a Catalyst in Political Finance

The integration of AGI and ChatGPT in the realm of political contributions marks a pivotal shift in political engagement, echoing the transformative impact seen in Enterprise GlobeTaste Bistro's operations. These technologies promise to bring about a future in political finance where contributions are more strategic, impactful, and aligned with individual and organizational values. As we venture into this new era, political finance is reimagined through the lens of AI, setting the stage for a more informed, transparent, and effective political landscape.

106

Section 2: Vision Paper: Transformative Impact of AGI and ChatGPT in Political Participation
Case (2): Ballot Helper – Revolutionizing Voter Engagement in the USA with AI
The "Enterprise GlobeTaste Bistro" Paradigm

Section 2: Vision Paper: Transformative Impact of AGI and ChatGPT in Political Participation

Case (2): Ballot Helper – Revolutionizing Voter Engagement in the USA with AI

Introduction: Empowering the Electorate in the Digital Age

In the context of the United States' political system, where voter engagement and informed decision-making are paramount, the advent of Artificial General Intelligence (AGI) and ChatGPT opens new avenues for empowering voters. This vision paper explores the potential of these technologies to revolutionize the voting process, providing American citizens with enhanced tools for understanding ballots, issues, and candidates, akin to the customer-centric innovations witnessed at Enterprise GlobeTaste Bistro.

I. General Impact of AGI and ChatGPT in Voter Engagement:

- **Informed Voting Decisions:** AGI can analyze complex legislative measures, candidate platforms, and political data, presenting voters with clear, unbiased information to aid their decision-making process.

- **Personalized Voter Assistance:** ChatGPT, with its natural language processing capabilities, can offer personalized guidance to voters, answering questions about ballot measures, election procedures, and candidate positions in an easy-to-understand format.

II. Relation to Enterprise GlobeTaste Bistro's Technologies:

- **Customized Information Delivery:** Just as Enterprise GlobeTaste Bistro utilizes AGI to tailor dining experiences, AGI can be employed to provide voters with customized information based on their interests, concerns, and the specifics of their local ballots.

- **Interactive Voter Education:** Drawing from ChatGPT's role in engaging customers at the Bistro, this technology can create interactive, educational experiences for voters, helping them navigate the complexities of ballots and political issues with ease.

III. Enhancing Voter Participation and Democracy:

- **Breaking Down Barriers to Voting:** By simplifying the understanding of ballots and the voting process, AGI and ChatGPT can help reduce barriers to voting, particularly for first-time voters or those who find the political process intimidating.
- **Promoting Informed Participation:** These technologies can contribute to a more informed electorate, ensuring that voters have access to the information they need to participate fully in the democratic process.

IV. Impact on Election Transparency and Integrity:

- **Transparent Information Dissemination:** AGI and ChatGPT can serve as tools for disseminating accurate and unbiased information about candidates and issues, promoting transparency in the electoral process.

- **Countering Misinformation:** By providing factual and easily accessible information, these AI technologies can play a crucial role in countering misinformation and ensuring that voters have reliable sources of information.

V. Conclusion: AI as a Pillar of Democratic Engagement

The integration of AGI and ChatGPT as ballot helpers in the United States marks a significant advancement in democratic engagement. These technologies promise a future where voters are better equipped to navigate the electoral process, making informed decisions based on comprehensive, personalized, and unbiased information. As we move towards this future, the role of AI in enhancing democratic participation becomes increasingly pivotal, echoing the customer-centric approach of Enterprise GlobeTaste Bistro in revolutionizing the culinary experience.

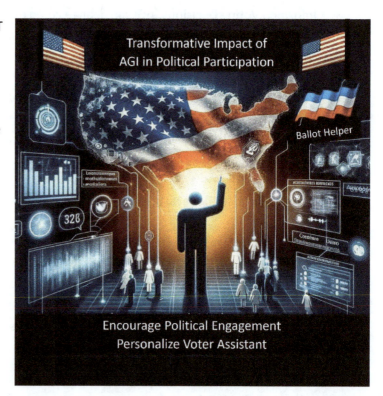

108

Section III: Vision Paper: Transformative Impact of AGI and ChatGPT in Community Support
Case (3): Mutual Aid Services and Immigration Aid in the USA –
AI-Driven Community Assistance
The "Enterprise GlobeTaste Bistro" Paradigm

Section III: Vision Paper: Transformative Impact of AGI and ChatGPT in Community Support
Case (3): Mutual Aid Services and Immigration Aid in the USA – AI-Driven Community Assistance

Introduction: Enhancing Community Support Through Technology

In an era where community support and assistance are increasingly vital, particularly in contexts like immigration aid in the USA, the advent of Artificial General Intelligence (AGI) and ChatGPT heralds a new phase of AI-driven assistance. This vision paper explores how these technologies can revolutionize mutual aid services, offering unparalleled support and guidance to those navigating the complex landscape of immigration and community assistance, reflecting the customer-focused innovations seen at Enterprise GlobeTaste Bistro.

I. General Impact of AGI and ChatGPT in Mutual Aid Services:

- **Comprehensive Assistance and Guidance:** AGI can process vast amounts of legal and regulatory information, providing up-to-date guidance on immigration laws, procedures, and resources, similar to how it manages complex culinary data at the Bistro.

- **Personalized Support for Immigrants:** ChatGPT can interact with individuals seeking immigration aid, offering personalized assistance based on their specific circumstances and queries, akin to the tailored customer service at the Bistro.

II. Relation to Enterprise GlobeTaste Bistro's Technologies:

- **Customized Information Delivery:** Just as AGI at the Bistro customizes dining experiences based on customer preferences, AGI in mutual aid services can tailor information and resources to meet the specific needs of individuals seeking immigration aid.

- **Responsive and Interactive Communication:** Leveraging ChatGPT's capabilities for interactive and responsive communication, mutual aid services can provide real-time assistance, answering questions and offering support in a conversational manner.

III. Enhancing Accessibility and Equity in Aid Services:

- **Breaking Down Barriers to Access:** AGI and ChatGPT can help simplify complex information and procedures, making immigration aid more accessible to diverse communities, including those with limited legal knowledge or language barriers.
- **Promoting Inclusivity and Fairness:** By providing accurate and personalized information, these technologies can contribute to a more equitable and inclusive approach to immigration aid and community support.

IV. Impact on Community Integration and Support:

- **Facilitating Community Integration:** AI-driven aid services can assist immigrants in understanding their rights, accessing resources, and integrating into communities, enhancing their overall well-being and participation in society.

- **Building Stronger Communities:** By supporting individuals in need, these technologies can strengthen community bonds and foster a sense of solidarity and mutual support.

V. Conclusion: AI as a Catalyst for Compassionate Community Support

The integration of AGI and ChatGPT in mutual aid and immigration services in the USA represents a significant step forward in community support. These technologies promise a future where assistance is more accessible, personalized, and effective, ensuring that individuals navigating the complexities of immigration receive the help they need. As we move towards this future, the role of AI in enhancing community support and building stronger, more inclusive societies becomes increasingly essential, mirroring the personalized and responsive approach of Enterprise GlobeTaste Bistro in the culinary domain.

110

Conclusion to the Series: Envisioning an AI-Enhanced Future in Societal Engagement

As this series of vision papers concludes, we stand at the cusp of a transformative era where the capabilities of Artificial General Intelligence (AGI) and ChatGPT are extending their reach beyond the confines of commercial enterprises, permeating the very fabric of societal engagement and civic participation. The examples set in the domains of political finance, voter assistance, and community support represent pioneering steps towards a broader, more inclusive narrative - one where AI acts as a catalyst for empowerment, equity, and efficiency in various facets of societal life.

Comprehensive Transformation Across Civic and Community Arenas

The integration of AGI and ChatGPT in the realms explored in this series marks the beginning of a revolutionary shift in how we interact with political systems, engage in the democratic process, and support our communities. It's a shift from traditional, often cumbersome processes to more streamlined, accessible, and personalized experiences, much like the transformation witnessed at Enterprise GlobeTaste Bistro in the culinary industry.

- **In Political Finance:** The role of AI in political contribution advising is not merely about optimizing donations but about fostering a more transparent, informed, and participatory political landscape. It's about enabling individuals and organizations to contribute to the political discourse in ways that align with their values and aspirations, thereby enhancing the democratic fabric of society.

- **In Voter Engagement:** The application of AI in ballot assistance underscores a commitment to strengthening democracy. By demystifying the voting process and providing accessible information on ballots and candidates, AGI and ChatGPT are tools that can drive higher voter turnout and more informed decision-making, key pillars of a vibrant democratic system.

- **In Community Support:** In the context of immigration aid and mutual aid services, AI emerges as a powerful ally in breaking down barriers, providing critical information, and facilitating access to essential services. This use of technology embodies a compassionate approach to community assistance, where support is not just available but is tailored to the unique needs and circumstances of each individual.

A Future Shaped by Collaborative Intelligence

The future envisioned in this series is one where AI is not a distant, impersonal force but a collaborative partner that enhances human capabilities and augments our potential to create more inclusive and equitable societies. This future is not just a possibility but an emerging reality, marking the

111

dawn of an era where every facet of societal engagement is reimagined and revitalized through the power of AGI and ChatGPT.

Invitation to Embrace a World of AI-Driven Societal Empowerment

As we conclude, we invite stakeholders from all sectors - political, social, and community-focused - to envision and embrace this AI-enhanced future. It's a future where technology empowers individuals and communities, making civic participation more meaningful and community support more impactful. In this new era, every initiative, whether aimed at influencing political discourse or providing community aid, is a step towards a smarter, more empathetic, and more sustainable society, driven by the synergistic collaboration of AI and human insight.

About the Book
World Bistro Enterprise: Gourmet Genius Evolution

"World Bistro Enterprise: Gourmet Genius Evolution" offers a visionary exploration into the transformative impact of Artificial General Intelligence (AGI) and ChatGPT across multiple industries, with a particular focus on the culinary sector. This book encapsulates the dawn of a new enterprise era, where AI technologies are no longer mere tools but fundamental drivers of innovation, efficiency, and strategic foresight across the global business landscape.

The narrative begins with the Enterprise GlobeTaste Bistro, a pioneering example of how AI can revolutionize traditional business models, creating a seamless integration of AI-driven operational efficiencies and personalized customer experiences. This model not only redefines culinary arts but also serves as a scalable blueprint for other industries, including healthcare, finance, education, and retail, illustrating the broad potential of AGI and ChatGPT to transcend industry boundaries and enhance business operations.

Through a series of in-depth analyses and case studies, the book explores how these technologies foster a culture of data-driven decision-making and personalized service delivery. It delves into the specific applications of AGI and ChatGPT in streamlining processes such as inventory management, customer engagement, and strategic planning, highlighting the universal applicability of the Bistro's AI-driven approaches.

"World Bistro Enterprise (Gourmet Genius Evolution)" not only underscores the critical role of AI in modern business practices but also projects a future where AI and human creativity coalesce to unlock new realms of possibility. This vision paper invites readers to envision a world where every industry leverages AI to achieve unparalleled success and innovation, inspired by the trailblazing journey of the Enterprise GlobeTaste Bistro.

Introduction to the Book
World Bistro Enterprise: Gourmet Genius Evolution

At the vanguard of the new enterprise era, "World Bistro Enterprise: Gourmet Genius Evolution" serves as a profound testament to the transformative power of Artificial General Intelligence (AGI) and ChatGPT across varied industries. This book marks a significant epoch where the confluence of technology and everyday business operations catalyzes a broad spectrum revolution, not just within the confines of the culinary world but extending its reach to fundamentally reshape global commerce and industry interactions.

The narrative pivots around the innovative Enterprise GlobeTaste Bistro, a model of how deeply embedded AI technologies can redefine traditional business frameworks, leading to enhanced operational efficiency, strategic agility, and an unprecedented level of personalized customer experience. This establishment is not merely a restaurant but a microcosm of potential widespread transformations achievable when AGI and ChatGPT are integrated into the core fabric of business practices.

As we delve into this exploration, the book elucidates the symbiotic relationship between AI advancements and human creativity, heralding a new era where these tools transcend their auxiliary roles to become central to reengineering industry paradigms. From healthcare and finance to education and retail, the ripple effects of this integration promise a future rich with innovation, strategic prowess, and enhanced efficiency.

"World Bistro Enterprise: Gourmet Genius Evolution" invites readers to embark on a comprehensive journey, showcasing how the strategic application of AI technologies can lead to a reimagined world of business. This introduction sets the stage for an enlightening discourse on the future of industries energized by AI, positioning the Enterprise GlobeTaste Bistro not only as a harbinger of culinary innovation but also as a beacon for universal business transformation.

Concluding Remark
World Bistro Enterprise: Gourmet Genius Evolution

As we close the pages of "World Bistro Enterprise: Gourmet Genius Evolution," we are left with a compelling vision of a future shaped profoundly by the integration of Artificial General Intelligence (AGI) and ChatGPT. The transformative journey of the Enterprise GlobeTaste Bistro serves as a microcosm of the potential that these technologies hold for a wide array of industries. From enhancing culinary ventures to revolutionizing healthcare, finance, and education, the reach of AGI and ChatGPT extends far beyond mere automation, positioning these tools as central pillars in the redefinition of modern enterprises.

The narrative detailed in this book underscores not only the operational and strategic enhancements brought about by AI but also the potential for these technologies to foster a new ethos within business practices. It paints a future where business operations are not just efficient but also more attuned to the needs and expectations of consumers. The successes and innovations at Enterprise GlobeTaste Bistro provide a blueprint for other industries to emulate, suggesting that the judicious application of AI can lead to substantial gains in productivity, strategic insight, and customer satisfaction.

Moreover, "World Bistro Enterprise: Gourmet Genius Evolution" challenges us to think beyond the conventional applications of AI in business. It invites industry leaders, policymakers, and thinkers to envisage and craft a future that leverages AI to address complex challenges and enhance every facet of human endeavor. It is a call to action to harness the potential of AI not just for incremental change but for transformative, sustainable progress that resonates across all sectors of society.

In conclusion, the journey of Enterprise GlobeTaste Bistro stands not merely as a narrative of success but as a beacon for the limitless possibilities of an AI-driven future. It heralds a new era of industry, one characterized by a symbiotic blend of technology and human creativity, promising a landscape where businesses not only thrive but also contribute to a broader, more sustainable world. As we move forward, the insights from this book offer valuable lessons and inspirations for harnessing the power of AGI and ChatGPT to reshape the world's economic and social fabric.

About the Author
Dr. Masoud Nikravesh

Dr. Masoud Nikravesh is a world-renowned expert in the field of Artificial Intelligence (AI) and Machine Learning, boasting a rich career that spans over three decades, with a record of remarkable leadership in academia, government, and the industry. As an accomplished scholar, Dr. Nikravesh has contributed significantly to the body of knowledge in AI, authoring over 15 scientific books, over 500 research papers, over 100 Children's books, and including a nine-book mental health series and a seven-book novel series. His current work is focused on the development and execution of national AI strategies, underlining AI's pivotal role in society, economic development, national defense, and national security strategies.

Dr. Nikravesh has uniquely combined his AI expertise with creativity to produce the book series "Princess Austėja" and "The Enduring Legacy of the Five Tattooed Princesses" using AGI to generate captivating narratives. This innovative application of AI and AGI showcases its potential for creative expression beyond traditional domains.

This book is the result of a collaboration between author Masoud Nikravesh and AI technologies like ChatGPT & GPT4.

www.ingramcontent.com/pod-product-compliance
Lightning Source LLC
LaVergne TN
LVHW081659050326
832903LV00026B/1834